HUMBLE
FATHERHOOD

How to Embrace the Roles of Fatherhood and Lead with Love and Intention

JACK EVES

ISBN: 979-8-218-85761-5

Dedication

First and foremost, my deepest gratitude goes to my wife, Gina, the love of my life and my anchor. Gina, your unwavering support, encouragement, and belief in me have carried me through every step of this journey. You inspire me daily, and I am endlessly grateful to share this life with you.

To my incredible children—Natasha, Hayden, and Jackson—you are my pride and joy. You have each shaped me in ways you'll never fully know, and my work here is as much for you as it is a reflection of the love and inspiration you bring to my life.

To my mother, thank you for being the example of strength, resilience, and compassion that has guided me in becoming the man I am today. Your influence runs through every word on these pages.

Finally, a special thanks to my father, whose memory continues to be a guiding force in my life. Dad, you were everything I could have asked for in a role model and more. I miss our daily conversations and your steady, unwavering support. You taught me so much about fatherhood, integrity, and love. This book is, in many ways, a tribute to you and the profound influence you continue to have on my life. Thank you, Dad, I miss you every day.

TABLE OF CONTENTS

Introduction

The idea for this book began with a conversation at work.

My co-worker and I were discussing life and work when I began sharing stories from a unique job I held previously with a university. I had been given the opportunity to visit jails to teach fatherhood classes to justice-involved fathers. It was significant work. These men, despite their difficult circumstances, were thinking about their kids. They wanted to grow. They wanted to show up better. They were asking hard questions about what it means to be a good father.

As I shared those stories, Anthony, who was a younger man, wanted to know more. He began to ask his own questions—not about the job, but about fatherhood itself. *"What is it like to be a dad?"* he asked. That question opened a door. Soon our daily conversations were filled with more questions, like:

"How do you know you're ready to be a father?"

"What if you didn't grow up with a good example?"

"How do you lead with love, even when you're exhausted?"

Some of Anthony's questions I could answer on the spot. Others required more reflection. I began digging into my journals, my memories, and my own experiences as a father and classroom teacher. One thing became clear to me: these weren't just Anthony's questions; they were questions that many young men carry with them, quietly, heavily, often without a place to ask them out loud.

I had the privilege of having a good father. My dad was someone I could go to with my doubts and worries. He was present, steady, and full of quiet wisdom. When I had questions, I had someone I trusted to help me work through them. But over the years, I have realized how rare that is. So many young men grow up without a healthy father-son relationship. They carry father-shaped questions into adulthood with no one to answer them. That's what made these conversations with Anthony so important—and what ultimately led me to write this book.

Anthony was generous enough to share his story, which I share here, with his permission, in his own words:

"Thinking back on my childhood, I never had a solid father figure. My dad was always busy, either in school, working full time, or just trying to keep a roof over our heads. He worked incredibly hard for my well-being, but in return, I never really got to see him.

So, when my wife and I graduated and the next natural step was starting a family, fear seeped into me. The worry of being a bad husband was bad enough, but the thought of being a bad father was even more terrifying.

Around this time, I started talking with my co-worker Jack Eves at work. He explained how normal all of these questions and feelings were. He even typed up something for me that validated everything I was feeling. It was titled 'A Father's Hopes and Fears,' and reading it felt like Jack was reading my mind.

Jack helped me understand that the best thing I could do for my child, and for myself, is to just be there - to never give up on being a good dad."

Anthony's words remind me why this book matters. If he had these questions, others surely did, too.

This book isn't about having all the answers. It's about being honest. It's about sharing stories—some beautiful, some hard-earned—and offering them as a resource, a mirror, and a companion to any man walking into the most important job they'll ever have: fatherhood.

My hope is that this book will meet you where you are—whether you're expecting your first child, raising teenagers, or healing from the past. Wherever you stand, you are not alone. Let's walk this journey together.

CHAPTER
ONE

A Balancing Act
Hopes, Fears, and the Father's Roles

Becoming a father is a journey unlike any other. It marks the beginning of a profound transformation, where life's priorities shift, and a man steps into a role that will shape not only his children's future but also his own. Fatherhood is both exhilarating and daunting, filled with dreams of what could be and anxieties about what might come. The hopes a father holds for his children are boundless and often connected with deep-seated fears. This emotional division—hoping and striving for the best while dreading the unknown—presents the complexity and the balancing act that is Fatherhood.

At the core of fatherhood is hope—the dream that one's children will grow into happy, fulfilled individuals. From the moment of his child's birth, a father's foremost concern is for their health and well-being. Each milestone in his child's life— their first steps, first words, first days of school—fuels that hope, fostering dreams of a bright and successful future. Whether it is seeing them thrive academically, excel in a chosen career, or form meaningful relationships, every father envisions a future filled with joy, success, and fulfillment for his children. Yet, beyond these tangible achievements, there is a deeper hope that his children will grow into good, kind people, embodying values like compassion, integrity, and resilience.

This aspiration extends beyond just personal success. Fathers hope their children will contribute positively to the world, treating others with empathy and respect. In a world often overshadowed by negativity, this hope takes on greater importance—a desire to raise not just accomplished individuals but good, ethical human beings who stand up for what is right. The dream of fostering strong character is a legacy many fathers wish to pass on, believing it is one of the most valuable gifts they can give.

Alongside the hopes, however, come the inevitable fears. The weight of responsibility that fatherhood brings is immense, often accompanied by doubts and uncertainties. Fathers grapple with the anxiety of failure, questioning their ability to provide, guide, and protect their children. This apprehension can be overwhelming, as fathers wonder if they are doing enough to prepare their children for the complexities of life. The question, *"Am I raising them the right way?"* can linger, especially during challenging times, keeping fathers awake at night as they reflect on their own perceived shortcomings.

Perhaps one of the most profound dreads is the fear of the unknown. Life is unpredictable, and no matter how much a father wants to shield his children from pain or disappointment, there are things beyond his control. From the day a child takes their first steps to the day they leave home, the world presents countless risks. Fathers constantly worry about their children's safety, hoping they will remain unscathed by physical danger and the harsh realities of life. This unease is ever-present, sometimes quietly tucked away, but always lurking in the background.

Fathers also contend with societal pressure that comes with the roles they are supposed to play. The modern father is expected to be both the traditional provider and the emotional nurturer, balancing work responsibilities with an active presence in the home. This dual role can create an internal struggle, as fathers strive to meet both sets of expectations. The uneasiness of not living up to these standards and not being enough in either role can weigh heavily.

Additionally, fathers often worry about the inevitable changes in their relationships with their children as they grow. As children become more independent and forge their own identities, there is a natural shift in the parent-child dynamic. Fathers may worry about becoming distant or irrelevant in their children's lives, fearing that the emotional connections they worked so hard to build might fade. This apprehension is often compounded by the realization that, as children grow, their need for parental guidance diminishes, making the dread of losing that connection even more real.

Then there is the existential unease: What legacy will a father leave behind? Will his values, his lessons, and his love endure in his children's lives long after he is gone? This concern often goes unspoken but is deeply felt. Fathers worry whether the love they poured into their children will resonate and whether the lessons of kindness and perseverance will be remembered and carried forward.

Navigating the hopes and fears of fatherhood requires patience and reflection. It is a delicate balance—dreaming big for a child's future while remaining ever vigilant in the face of life's uncertainties. Yet, within this balance lies the essence of fatherhood. A father's love drives him to keep hoping, keep dreaming, and keep striving, even in the face of dread.

Parenthood often brings to light the differing approaches each parent has when it comes to balancing work and family responsibilities. This delicate balance can be one of the most challenging aspects of raising children, as parents juggle their careers while trying to maintain a meaningful presence at home. Each parent may have a unique perspective on how to manage these dual roles, shaped by personal values, experiences, and societal expectations. These differences, while natural, can sometimes lead to tension as parents navigate the complex dynamics of family life.

Historically, fathers were primarily seen as breadwinners, while mothers took on the role of caregivers. But today, these traditional roles have evolved, with both parents often sharing responsibilities at home and in the workplace. In many households, fathers are more involved in child-rearing than in previous generations, while mothers are increasingly pursuing careers. This shift has created new dynamics in how families function, but it has also introduced new challenges. While one parent may focus on professional success, the other may prioritize being emotionally and physically present at home, leading to different expectations about how to balance the demands of work and family life.

Communication becomes crucial in navigating these differences. Both parents must express their needs, share their concerns, and find a way to support one another. Whether it is agreeing who takes on certain household responsibilities or finding ways to be more present for their children, parents need to work as a team. Striking the right balance requires flexibility, compromise, and a willingness to adapt as family dynamics and career demands change.

Understanding and respecting each other's approaches is key to maintaining a harmonious household. Ultimately, the goal is not to eliminate these differences but to find a balance that allows both parents to thrive in their roles, creating a nurturing environment for their children while still achieving their personal and professional goals.

When I first found out I was going to be a dad, I was flooded with excitement, but even more so, apprehension. I always thought that fatherhood was something I would take on when I was "ready," but suddenly, there I was, facing the reality that I had no idea what that meant. The truth was, I did not feel equipped. I questioned if I had what it took to be a good dad. What if I messed it all up? What if I was not patient enough, strong enough, or even loving enough?

In the months leading up to my daughter's birth, I was haunted by feelings of inadequacy. I saw other dads who seemed to have it all together—the way they balanced everything, how they always seemed to know what to do. I was afraid that I didn't have what it took to provide the kind of life my child deserved. I felt lost.

But then the day came. The moment I first held my daughter in my arms is a moment I'll never forget. It felt like time stopped. There she was, so small, so fragile, and yet so perfect. I could feel her warmth, her little chest rising and falling as she took her first breaths in the world. And in that instant, all my insecurities melted away.

I remember looking down at her tiny face, her little fingers wrapped around mine, and suddenly I felt this overwhelming sense of peace. It was like nothing else in the world mattered anymore. Everything I had dreaded about not being enough, about not knowing what to do—just faded away. I was her father, and somehow, in that moment, I felt like I was on top of the world.

It wasn't just the pride or the joy, though those were there too. It was this deep, unshakable connection. She was a part of me, and I knew, at that moment, I would do whatever it took to give her the best life I could.

But soon after, the worries crept back in. Would I be able to teach her the things she needed to know? Would I be patient and understanding when she struggled? I began questioning myself again—how could I ever be enough for her? How could I be the dad she deserved?

I lay awake some nights wondering about her future, hoping that I could be the kind of father who could support her dreams, guide her through challenges, and be her safe place. The responsibility felt enormous. I wanted to protect her from every hardship, but I also knew that she would have to face her struggles, and all I could do was be there for her.

Over time, I've come to realize that being a good dad isn't about having all the answers or being perfect. It's about showing up, being present, and doing the best you can every day. I've made mistakes, and I'm sure I'll make plenty more, but each day I learn something new about being her father.

Every smile, every laugh, and even the tears have taught me more about myself than I could have imagined. And though I may never fully shake the unease that I might not be enough, I know that my love for her is endless—and that's what matters most.

TWO

The Shield
A Father's Duty as Protector

One warm summer, with our daughter just four years old and our son barely two, we set off for a family camping adventure on Utah's Kolob Mountain. The day couldn't have been better fishing in the cool mountain air, hiking trails that seemed to stretch forever, and finishing the evening with barbecue chicken grilled over the fire. The kids were sticky-fingered, happy, and exhausted by bedtime, which meant we were in for a peaceful night. Or so we thought. Sometime after midnight, I woke to a strange sound inside the tent. At first, I thought I was imagining it — a soft, persistent licking. And then, I looked over and nearly lost my mind: perched right on my son's chest was a skunk, happily licking the barbecue sauce off his tiny fingers.

Panic surged through me. My first instinct was to move, to grab my son and shoo the skunk away — but I knew that any sudden movement could provoke the animal. I froze, my heart pounding, and quietly nudged my wife awake. Through whispering words, we coordinated our response: she threw a blanket over the kids, and herself. Startled, the skunk scampered out of the tent leaving all of us unharmed, and thankfully, unsprayed.

As we exhaled and laughed nervously, the absurdity of the situation hit me. Here I was, a father, supposed to be the protector, facing off against one of nature's most notorious little villains — armed with nothing but a blanket and a cool head. My children, blissfully asleep through the whole ordeal, didn't even notice the adventure.

That night, I realized something important about a father's duty. Protection isn't always about grand gestures or heroic battles; sometimes it's about staying calm under pressure, thinking quickly, and finding creative solutions — all while keeping your children safe. And sometimes, it's about embracing the absurdity of life, laughing at the chaos, and knowing that even in the wildest moments, you're there to shield them from harm.

Kolob Mountain gave me a story I'll never forget, but more importantly, it reminded me that fatherhood is full of surprises. Some are messy, some are funny, and some—like a skunk on your toddler's chest—test your nerves in ways you never imagined. And through it all, the job of a father remains the same: to be the shield, the calm in the storm, and the steady hand guiding your child, even when the world gets a little...stinky.

When a child enters the world, a father assumes the role of protector. He is a guardian who fosters an unshakable sense of security in the child's life. This security goes beyond simply keeping the child safe from physical harm. It is about creating an environment where the child feels confident to explore, knowing they are protected both physically and emotionally. A father's protective presence, whether through daily interactions or the unspoken assurance of support, builds the foundation of trust and safety that shapes a child's understanding of the world.

To ensure this sense of security, a father must be both physically present and emotionally available, providing consistency, reliability, and nurturing guidance. In doing so, he lays the groundwork for his child's healthy development, offering them not only protection but also the tools to become resilient and self-assured individuals.

At the heart of every child's sense of security is the knowledge that their parents or guardians will keep them safe. From infancy, a father's role as protector is visible in the most basic ways—babyproofing the house, ensuring the crib is secure, and gently cradling the newborn to sleep. As the child grows, the forms of protection evolve. Whether it is teaching them to cross the street safely, supervising their first bike ride, or coaching them through their first emergency, the father's protective instincts are ever-present. He teaches his children how to navigate the physical world with caution and confidence, instilling lessons that will stay with them throughout life.

Yet, protection is not just about sheltering the child from immediate dangers, it is about preparing them for the harsher realities of the world. A father knows that one day his child will have to face challenges on their own. By teaching them how to respond to danger, how to think critically, and how to overcome crises calmly, he lays the foundation for a self-reliant adult. In this way, the father's protection extends beyond the present, equipping his child with the skills they need to thrive in an unpredictable world—knowing they can always rely on him as a safety net when needed.

A father's role as protector extends into the emotional landscape of a child's life. A father who listens attentively, offers a comforting hug, or simply shows up during tough moments provides a child with a sense of emotional safety. This emotional security is built on trust—the trust that the father will be there, no matter what curve balls life throws at them.

Children seek reassurance from their fathers in countless ways, whether they are coping with fears, uncertainties, or disappointments. The comfort of a father's presence during these moments, his ability to listen without judgment, and his unwavering support help the child feel valued and understood. This consistency forms the bedrock of emotional security, allowing the child to express their feelings freely and develop healthy relationships with others. The knowledge that their father will stand by them, offering guidance and love, creates a powerful sense of emotional stability.

A vital part of ensuring a child's sense of security is establishing clear boundaries—rules and structures that provide predictability in their world. Children thrive when they know what is expected of them and when their environment is structured and supportive. Fathers play a crucial role in setting these boundaries, enforcing rules with love and fairness, and helping their children navigate the consequences of their actions.

Boundaries are not meant to restrict; rather, they create a safe space within which a child can explore the world. Fathers who establish these limits help their children develop self-discipline, responsibility, and a sense of accountability. Within the framework of these boundaries, children learn the importance of making choices and understanding the impact of their decisions. The security of knowing that their father's guidance is always rooted in care gives children the confidence to grow and develop a healthy sense of self-esteem.

Children often look to their fathers for comfort and reassurance, especially during times of fear or uncertainty. Whether it is soothing them after a bad dream, offering encouragement during a difficult day at school, or helping them manage their anxieties about growing up, a father's comforting presence is a powerful force in a child's life. Fathers who consistently provide this emotional security give their children the confidence to face life's challenges head on.

By reassuring their children that it is okay to be afraid and that failure is a part of life, fathers help their children develop a healthy attitude toward adversity. They learn that setbacks are not permanent and that they can always find strength from their family support system. Over time, this consistent reassurance helps children build the confidence they need to face obstacles with courage, knowing they are never alone and that they can overcome challenges.

Ultimately, a father's greatest gift to his child is the sense of security that comes from love and connectedness. This bond is formed through shared experiences—spending quality time together, engaging in meaningful activities, and showing interest in the child's thoughts and feelings. Whether it is playing together, teaching new skills, or standing by them during difficult moments, a father's active involvement in his child's life creates a depth of connection that fosters a profound sense of security. A child who feels this deep sense of security carries it with them throughout their life, impacting how they form relationships, approach challenges, and view the world.

In this nurturing environment, children are free to dream, take risks, and face life's challenges, knowing that their father is always there to guide and protect them. Fathers who embrace this role leave behind not only memories of love but a legacy of security that shapes their children's future, allowing them to navigate the world with confidence and courage.

From the moment I became a father, the overwhelming feeling that struck me was the instinct to protect. Protecting my children, both physically and emotionally, became my greatest purpose and my greatest fear. But even though I knew in my heart that I would do anything for them, I often questioned whether I was strong enough for the job. I wondered if I could truly shield them from the harshness of the world, to be their first line of defense in a life that can sometimes be unpredictable and unforgiving. I wanted to be the rock they could always rely on, but at times, I felt more like sand, unsure if I was solid enough to give them the protection they needed.

I watched other fathers, ones who seemed so confident in their role, and I wondered how they did it. How did they stay calm when their child was struggling? How did they always seem to know the right thing to say, the perfect way to make things better? In those moments of doubt, I feared I was falling short. The weight of fatherhood felt like a burden I wasn't fully prepared for, even though I loved my children more than anything in this world.

There were times when I felt inadequate, moments when I doubted my ability to be the protector they deserved. When they were sick, scared, or hurt, I would rush to comfort them, but deep down, I questioned if my efforts and skills were enough. Every fever, every scraped knee, and every time they came to me with tears in their eyes I wondered, was I doing this right? Could I give them the sense of safety they needed?

Once when I was 300 miles away at a conference for work, my oldest son became sick. His mother was taking care of him, but his condition continued to worsen regardless. I felt helpless being so far away. All I could do was check in constantly, hoping for updates, but each call left me more anxious. His fever wasn't breaking, and his energy was fading. I wanted to be there to hold him and reassure him that everything would be okay, but I couldn't.

Even after returning home, I was still anxious, because my son was not getting better. My wife and I decided to take him to the doctor again because we felt like something was seriously wrong. The doctor couldn't figure out what was going on, but he also suspected it could be something more than a regular illness. At this point, my wife insisted that they send our son to the hospital for a scan of his abdomen. All we could do was trust that the doctors were making the right decisions, but I was terrified.

Eventually, the call came from the hospital that they had found the issue—appendicitis that had already ruptured. My heart sank. I felt like I had failed as a father. I should have come home sooner; I should have known the illness was more than just a fever.

My son needed to go into surgery to have his burst appendix removed. Watching him disappear behind those hospital doors was one of the hardest moments of my life. The surgery felt like it lasted forever. Every second that passed, I was consumed by worry and guilt. I kept thinking, "What if I hadn't come back in time? What if we had waited longer to get him checked?" It was agonizing.

Finally, the doctor came out and told us that the surgery had been successful. Relief flooded over me, but it was mixed with the knowledge that this was just the beginning of my son's recovery. His appendix had ruptured days earlier, and the infection had spread. The road to recovery would be long, and the doctors warned us it could take some time for him to fully heal.

Even though the worst was over, watching my son struggle in those first few days post-surgery was almost unbearable. He was so small, so fragile, and it broke my heart to see him in pain. But I knew I had to stay strong for him, even though inside, I still questioned whether I had done enough. I stayed by his side as much as possible, helping him through the discomfort, encouraging him when it hurt to move, and doing everything I could to be there for him.

There were tough moments—nights when I'd sit beside his bed, watching him sleep, wondering if I could have done something to catch this sooner. But seeing my son's determination to get better reminded me that being a father isn't about being perfect or knowing all the answers. It's about being there, even in the moments when you feel helpless.

The months that followed were filled with ups and downs, but my son slowly regained his health. Little by little he was able to move around more, and I could see his energy coming back. There were setbacks, and it took longer than we hoped, but eventually, he fully recovered.

Looking back, that experience changed me as a father. It taught me that no matter how much we want to protect our children from everything, sometimes we can't. Sometimes all we can do is be there—to hold them, to comfort them, to let them know they aren't facing the world alone. In those moments, when I doubted my ability to be the protector he needed, I realized that showing up, staying by his side, and loving him through it all was what mattered most.

Of course, my son made it through, and so did I. He fought through his recovery with a strength I will always admire. And as hard as it was, I learned that being a father means facing those terrifying moments head-on, even when you don't feel like you're enough, because your love and presence are what make all the difference.

That's when I realized: *I was enough.*

The truth is, I've learned that I can't always protect them from everything. That realization was hard to accept at first. I always imagined that being a great father meant keeping them from every harm, but life doesn't work that way. Instead, I've had to learn that my job as a father is to teach them how to face the world's challenges, even when I'm not there to shield them, or when I feel scared or unequipped myself. Even in those moments of uncertainty, I remind myself that being a protector means standing by their side no matter what.

In the end, being a great father isn't about never feeling inadequate. It's about acknowledging those doubts and showing up anyway. It's about finding strength even when you feel weak. It's about realizing that your presence, your love, and your endless effort to protect them—even when you feel like you fall short—are what make you enough.

CHAPTER
THREE
The Teacher and Mentor
Nurturing Developing Minds

One of the most important roles a father undertakes is that of a teacher guide who passes on values and morals that will help shape his children's view of the world. These lessons become the foundation upon which a child builds their understanding of right and wrong, how to navigate complex situations, and how to live with purpose and integrity.

As a father, every decision you make, and every action you take, leaves an imprint on the hearts and minds of your children, creating a legacy that lasts far beyond your years. Children are like sponges, soaking up the behaviors and actions they see, especially from their parents. As the saying goes, "Actions speak louder than words," and nothing could be truer when it comes to parents teaching their children values.

Whether it is honesty, kindness, responsibility, or integrity, children learn these traits not through lectures, but by watching how you live. When you consistently do the right thing, even when no one is watching, you are showing them what it means to live with integrity. Your patience and respect in relationships, your kindness toward others, and your calmness under pressure all become living examples of the values you hope to pass on.

Teaching through everyday action offers a new opportunity to teach your children about values simply by the way you carry yourself. When you treat others with kindness, manage stressful situations with grace, and demonstrate honesty even when it is difficult, your children are learning those values, too. They watch how you navigate the world—how you deal with frustrations, how you comfort those who are hurting, and how you face challenges. Without saying a word, you are showing them how to stay strong, compassionate, and true to their principles in a world that often minimizes or even mocks those values.

However, it is not enough to assume that children will automatically know what is right or wrong just by observing. Parents must take an active role in engaging their children in conversations about values, explaining the "why" behind their decisions, and discussing the importance of morals in everyday life. Real-life examples, whether drawn from individual experiences or current events, can be powerful tools for sparking these conversations. Asking children how they would manage certain dilemmas or allowing them to question and explore moral concepts helps them develop their understanding and builds a sound ethical compass.

As a father, you are not just handing down rules, you are helping your children understand why those rules exist. This means encouraging them to ask questions, to think critically about choices, and to explore the consequences of actions. By fostering an environment where they can discuss and reason through moral issues, you are helping them develop independent thinking rooted in firm values. Life is full of tough choices, and by guiding your children through these decisions, you teach them that values like honesty, fairness, and kindness sometimes come with difficult but necessary sacrifices.

Children thrive when they understand what is expected of them. As a father, it is your job to establish rules that are grounded in the values you hold dear, while ensuring that those rules are communicated with love and consistency. Discipline, when done fairly and consistently, teaches children that actions have consequences. It is not about being strict for the sake of control, but about instilling a sense of responsibility, accountability, and fairness. As your children grow, they will need increasing levels of freedom, but this freedom should come with the expectation that they make choices in line with the values you have instilled.

The home environment, under your guidance, becomes the perfect setting to reinforce these shared family values. Whether through family rituals, traditions, or daily routines, fathers often set the tone for the household's moral compass. By creating a home where kindness, empathy, and respect are emphasized, you are helping your children absorb these values naturally.

Family traditions are a powerful way to reinforce values. Whether it is a weekly ritual of giving back to the community, practicing gratitude at the dinner table, or having regular discussions about respect and empathy, these shared activities leave a lasting impact. Praise also plays a significant role. When you celebrate moments of kindness, honesty, or courage within the family, you show your children that living by these values is both important and rewarding.

Teaching empathy is another critical aspect of your role as a father. Empathy—the ability to understand and share the feelings of others—forms the foundation for compassion and emotional intelligence. By modeling empathy in your interactions, whether by lending a helping hand to someone in need or showing patience in difficult situations, you are teaching your children to see the world from others' perspectives. Exposing your children to diverse cultures, lifestyles, and worldviews helps broaden their understanding and fosters a deeper sense of empathy.

Simple acts of service, such as volunteering or helping a neighbor, reinforce the idea that we are all part of a larger community and have a responsibility to care for others. These experiences help shape children into kind, compassionate individuals who are not only aware of the struggles of others but are also motivated to make a positive difference.

While core values are essential, life is rarely black and white. As your children grow, they will face situations that require flexibility, tolerance, and open-mindedness. Teaching them to navigate these gray areas with grace is a crucial part of your role as a father. Mistakes will be made, both by your children and by you. Teaching forgiveness, both for oneself and for others, is a lesson that will serve them throughout their lives. Showing them that it is okay to make mistakes but essential to learn from them helps your children understand the value of personal growth and accountability.

Perhaps one of the most important lessons a father can teach is humility. You are not perfect, and admitting your mistakes shows your children that being human means sometimes getting things wrong. More importantly, it demonstrates that taking responsibility for those mistakes and learning from them is what truly matters. Apologizing when you are wrong models humility and reinforces the importance of accountability. Sharing stories of your failures and the lessons they taught you helps your children understand that mistakes are part of life's learning process. It is not about avoiding failure but about how we rise from it that defines us.

Teaching values and morals is a lifelong journey that requires patience, intentionality, and reflection. Fathers serve as the guiding force, helping their children grow into kind, responsible, and ethical individuals. By living out the values you hope to instill, maintaining open communication, and fostering a family environment rooted in love and principles, you build a legacy that will guide your children through life's challenges and triumphs.

Beyond values, nurturing a love for learning is another crucial responsibility. As a father, you have the power to inspire a passion for education and intellectual curiosity in your children. Leading by example, demonstrating a love for lifelong learning, and actively engaging in educational activities with your children all contribute to shaping their attitude toward academics.

Ultimately, your influence as a father reaches far beyond the present moment. You are shaping how your children view the world, how they interact with it, and how they contribute to it. Through your teaching, your values will live on, not only in your children but in future generations as well. Passing on values and morals is one of the most significant and enduring roles a father plays in his children's lives. It is not just about rules or lessons learned in a single moment; it is about how these guiding principles gradually shape a child's perspective, decisions, and sense of responsibility in the world.

As a father, the values you live by influence not only your actions but also the legacy you pass on to your children, shaping how they view right from wrong and how they navigate life's complexities. Take a moment and think about the values that are most important to you. These are not just ideas to be talked about; they need to be lived. Children are always absorbing not just what you say, but what you do. If you want your child to understand honesty, they must witness you being honest, especially in tricky situations where a lie might be easier. Integrity is not just about the big decisions; it is in the everyday choices you make when no one is looking. When your child sees you standing firm in your beliefs, even when it is hard, they learn what integrity looks like in practice.

How you interact with the people around you teaches your child about respect, empathy, and kindness. The way you manage stress, disappointment, and even failure can become lessons in perseverance. When you manage adversity with grace and patience, your child learns the invaluable lesson that life's challenges do not define you—how you respond to them does.

Still, modeling values is not enough on its own; open conversations are crucial. Children need to understand not just what to do, but why. Take the time to talk with your kids about the decisions you make and the principles behind them. Discuss real-life scenarios or current events and let them explore the gray areas where right and wrong might not be so clear-cut. These conversations help children develop their moral compass, allowing them to think critically about their choices.

Encourage them to ask questions, even hard ones. Let them challenge your views or consider alternative perspectives. By guiding them through these discussions, you are helping them form their values, rooted in a deep understanding of why certain principles matter.

When I first became a father, I was struck by the sheer weight of responsibility that came with it. Nothing truly prepares you for the moment when you realize that you are shaping not only a life but also a soul. Providing food, shelter, and safety is one thing, but guiding a child's heart and mind is something far greater. It dawned on me that I was not only a parent but also a teacher, a mentor, and the first example to my children of what it looks like to be a good person.

That realization was daunting. I often asked myself if I was up to the task. Would I have the patience to teach them right from wrong? Would they listen when I tried to show them why kindness or honesty mattered? The responsibility felt heavy because I knew the lessons I taught—or failed to teach—would echo throughout their lives.

One of the earliest lessons I remember giving was about something as simple as not running into the road. Children are naturally curious, and their sense of danger is almost nonexistent. I can still recall the terror of watching one of my little ones dash toward the street, my heart nearly stopping as I pulled them back. At that moment, I explained why we had rules, why stopping to look and listen was non-negotiable. At first, it was just about safety, but over time it became something more. They were learning that boundaries were not meant to trap them but to protect them. Rules were not about control; they were about care.

As my children grew, these boundaries expanded into values. Our home became the classroom where lessons of honesty, respect, and compassion were practiced day by day. We built small rituals that turned into traditions: pausing before meals to share what we were grateful for, volunteering together in the community, and holding weekly conversations where everyone had the chance to be heard. These weren't grand gestures, but they carried meaning. They gave my children a sense that values are not abstract ideas; they are lived experiences, woven into the rhythm of family life.

And when someone displayed those values, maybe showing kindness to a sibling, or having the courage to admit a mistake, I celebrated it. Not in a way that made them feel like they were performing for approval, but in a way that reminded them that goodness is something to be attained and cherished. I wanted them to see that having character is beautiful.

Of course, much of what children learn doesn't come from lectures or rules; it comes from observation. They notice how we speak when we are frustrated, how we treat people when no one is watching, and how we respond when life doesn't go our way. I realized early on that if I wanted my children to grow into people of integrity, I needed to model it myself. That didn't mean perfection...far from it. In fact, some of the most meaningful lessons came from the times I failed.

There were moments when I lost my temper or made a choice I regretted. In those times, I tried to be honest. I apologized, explained what I had done wrong, and admitted that even fathers make mistakes. Far from weakening their trust, it increased it. My children saw that accountability is not about being flawless, but about taking responsibility. They learned that success is not the absence of failure, but the courage to face it, make amends, and move forward.

As my children grew older, sibling conflicts became one of the most challenging and, oddly, rewarding arenas for teaching. Arguments flared over toys, space, or misunderstandings. My instinct was always to jump in and solve the problem, but I realized that doing so robbed them of the opportunity to learn conflict resolution themselves. Instead, I guided them toward listening, toward expressing their frustrations without cruelty, and toward forgiveness. It wasn't always pretty, but slowly they learned that relationships aren't about keeping score or winning battles. They are about respect, empathy, and compromise.

I remember a time when one of my children said something hurtful to their sibling. Instead of scolding, I sat down and asked how they would feel if the same words were said to them. It wasn't about guilt-tripping, it was about helping them see things from someone else's perspective. It took time, but eventually, they began to understand the importance of treating others, especially family, with kindness.

Fatherhood also taught me the importance of flexibility. Life is rarely neat, and values, while foundational, often meet situations that test their boundaries. It is one thing to say, "Honesty is always best," but quite another to navigate moments when truth and compassion collide. It is one thing to believe in fairness, but another to guide a child through a situation where fairness doesn't seem to exist. Those are the moments when values like tolerance, open-mindedness, and forgiveness matter most. I want my children to know that it is possible to hold powerful convictions while still respecting those who see the world differently, and that forgiveness for self and others is a gift that frees the heart.

Passing on values is not a task to complete but a journey to walk. It is ongoing, requiring patience, reflection, and a willingness to keep learning as we go. I've come to see that as much as I am shaping my children, they are shaping me. They push me to examine my own values more closely, to live more consistently with what I say I believe.

Being a teacher and mentor is less about perfection and more about presence. It is about showing up again and again to guide, to model, to admit mistakes, and to celebrate growth. The values we embody will ripple outward through our children's lives, shaping not only who they become, but also the legacy they pass on to the next generation.

When I think about my daughter Natasha, my firstborn, I feel a profound sense of pride and love. She was my first experience of parenthood, the one who taught me as much as I taught her, and watching her grow has been one of the greatest joys of my life. I am awestruck by her wisdom, her independence, and her deep-rooted commitment to her values. From a young age, she has carried herself with integrity and a belief that the decisions she makes are an extension of who she is.

Natasha has become a young woman who not only values hard work and education but has learned to trust herself along the way. She grew from a curious child with endless questions to a confident young adult who navigates life with purpose and self-assurance, and it has been a privilege to watch.

As she got older, Natasha began working part-time jobs, managing her own time and finances. She took pride in earning her own money, knowing she could support herself in small but meaningful ways. This wasn't just about financial independence; it was about proving to herself that she could set goals and achieve them on her terms. The confidence that came from these experiences strengthened her, giving her a self-assuredness that no one could take away. Her sense of self allowed her to approach decisions with a calm confidence that has become one of her defining traits.

Natasha knew that her character was shaped not only by what she chose to do, but also by what she chose *not* to do. She began making choices based on what felt right for her, not just what others expected of her. This independence has shown in big and small ways—whether she's choosing friends, managing her schedule, or planning her future. She knows that while advice and guidance are valuable, she has the wisdom within herself to make the decisions that are best for her.

Education has come to mean much more than academic achievement for Natasha; it has become a way of learning about herself and the world, a way to learn how to stand on her own. She sees challenges as learning opportunities and treats setbacks as steppingstones. Each lesson, each job, and each choice has built within her an unshakeable foundation of self-trust, something I know will carry her through life's many stages.

My daughter's journey has only just begun, but her values—integrity, hard work, and confidence—will guide her every step of the way. She has become someone who knows who she is, trusts her decisions, and stands firm in her beliefs, and I have no doubt she will continue to lead her own life with courage and a heart full of purpose.

These are the moments that reassure me that I've done something right. I may not have all the answers, but I've learned that being a teacher to your children isn't about being perfect, it's about being present, leading by example, and helping them find their own way in the world with the right values to guide them.

CHAPTER
FOUR
The Playful Dad
The Importance of Play in Fatherhood

Play is the language of childhood. Through it, children explore the world, develop essential skills, and build lasting connections with those around them. For fathers, engaging in play with their children is not only a source of joy but a vital part of a child's overall development. While it may seem simple, play has profound effects on a child's cognitive, social, and emotional growth. As a father, being actively involved in play enhances your bond with your child and allows you to model critical life lessons in a way that feels natural and fun.

At first glance, play might appear to be just a way to keep kids entertained, but it serves as a foundation for much of their learning. Psychologists and educators agree that play is essential for developing critical thinking skills, creativity, emotional regulation, and social competencies.

Play stimulates brain development by encouraging children to think critically and solve problems in imaginative ways. Whether it is building a tower of blocks, navigating a board game, or creating an elaborate story with action figures, children learn to experiment with cause and effect, strategize, and develop their understanding of the world. Play can introduce concepts like fairness, competition, and taking turns, all of which are essential for later academic and life success.

Play is also a way for children to process emotions. Through role-playing or creative scenarios, children explore feelings like fear, frustration, happiness, and excitement in a safe environment. When fathers engage in these playful activities, they can help children navigate complex emotions, teaching them to regulate and express their feelings in healthy ways. This shared playtime creates opportunities to model empathy, patience, and resilience.

Interactive play between fathers and children encourages social skills like cooperation, communication, and conflict resolution. Whether playing catch in the backyard or teaming up for a puzzle, children learn to work alongside others, interpret nonverbal cues, and communicate effectively. Fathers who model respectful and kind interactions through play help their children practice these behaviors in real-world settings.

Active play is essential for physical development. Rough-and-tumble play, often more characteristic of father-child interactions, helps children develop motor skills, balance, and coordination. Moreover, it encourages risk-taking in a controlled environment, allowing children to push boundaries while feeling secure in their father's presence. Through playful wrestling, running, or sports, fathers help children understand their bodies and develop confidence in their physical abilities.

Research shows that fathers usually engage in play differently than mothers. Fathers tend to participate in more physically active play, while mothers may focus on nurturing or cooperative forms of play. Both styles are valuable, but a "rough housing" type of play, more often exhibited by fathers, has unique benefits for children. Fathers encourage their children to take risks during play—whether it is climbing higher on the jungle gym or trying out a new bike trick. This form of play teaches children to assess and manage risks in a safe environment. It builds confidence, teaches resilience, and helps children become comfortable with pushing their limits.

Rough-and-tumble play is not just about physical activity; it is a crucial way for children to learn about limitations and self-control. A father's playful wrestling or tickling provides an opportunity for children to assess their strengths, understand limits, and practice self-regulation. They learn that it is okay to lose sometimes, to fall, and to get back up again—important life lessons that help them cope with challenges later in life.

The playful interactions between fathers and their children are a key way to build emotional connections. Playtime becomes a space where children feel free to express themselves without fear of judgment, knowing that their father is fully present and engaged. This bonding fosters a sense of security and reinforces the father-child relationship. Children whose fathers play with them regularly feel valued and loved, reinforcing their self-esteem and sense of belonging.

Fathers often find it challenging to fit play into their busy schedules. However, even small moments of play can have a significant impact. Here are a few practical ways to engage in meaningful play with your child:

1. Incorporate physical play into your routine. Play catch, kick a soccer ball, or have a dance party in the living room. Active play promotes physical health and

provides a natural setting for teaching sportsmanship, perseverance, and teamwork.

2. Set aside dedicated time for play without distractions. Put your phone away, step away from work, and focus solely on your child. Even 20 minutes of undivided attention can create lasting memories and deepen your bond.

3. Let your child guide the play. Whether they want to pretend to be a superhero or create a make-believe tea party, allow them to take charge of the narrative. This encourages creativity and gives you insight into their interests and thought processes.

While it is important to set aside time for play, it doesn't always have to be confined to a specific time or place. By incorporating playfulness, you can make everyday activities more fun. Turn chores into a game, race your child to see who can put on their shoes faster, or tell a silly story during bath time. These small moments of joy contribute to a positive atmosphere in your home.

Do not be afraid to get silly! Whether your child wants you to be a dragon in a fantasy world or a customer at their make-believe store, dive into the role enthusiastically. This type of imaginative play helps children develop creativity, critical thinking skills, and emotional intelligence.

The benefits of father-child play extend far beyond childhood. Studies have shown that children who engage in regular play with their fathers are more likely to develop solid social skills, perform better academically, and have higher emotional intelligence. Fathers who play with their children also tend to have better, more open relationships with them during adolescence and adulthood.

Moreover, playful interactions teach children about healthy relationships, boundaries, and communication. As they grow, children will carry these lessons into their interactions with peers, teachers, and future partners. Fathers who prioritize play in their parenting set the foundation for their children to thrive in all aspects of life.

As a father, your role as a playmate is more than just entertainment—it is a powerful tool for shaping your child's development. Play offers a unique opportunity to connect with your child, build their confidence, and teach essential life skills naturally and enjoyably. Embrace the playful moments, no matter how small, and know that through play, you are giving your child the gift of your presence, guidance, and love.

I've come to realize that there's no greater privilege or responsibility than being a guiding force in your children's development. From the first moment I became a dad, I knew I wanted to be more than just a provider—I wanted to be actively involved in every step of my children's lives. What I didn't know at the time was how much that involvement, from the simplest games to the biggest milestones, would shape not only their development but mine as well.

One of the earliest memories I cherish with my daughter Natasha is playing with the Littlest Pet Shop and Polly Pocket toys with her. It may seem small to some, but for me, it was a way of stepping into her world and showing her that her interests mattered to me. I'd join her on the floor in this imaginative universe of make-believe, her tiny hands carefully arranging the miniature pets and setting up Polly's little world. Those moments were about more than just play, they were about connection, trust, and letting her know I was there for her, always.

As much as I loved those quiet, imaginative moments, there was always a balance of rough-and-tumble fun too. I'd swing Natasha around the backyard, her laughter echoing through the air, as we played on the swing set or jumped on the trampoline. My sons, on the other hand, loved to wrestle and roughhouse, and the backyard often turned into a mini-wrestling ring with the trampoline as the center stage. Natasha, of course, would jump in along with us, her joy radiating with each body slam.

The backyard wasn't just a playground—it was a place where laughter was shared and where each child learned about trust, boundaries, and fun. We built entire cities in the sandpile, digging out roads and tunnels, creating little worlds where our imaginations could run wild. I'd play catch with them, kicking the ball around, teaching them the joy of movement and the thrill of competition.

As they grew, so did our games. The little activities in the backyard turned into bigger sports: volleyball, baseball, football, and of course, more wrestling. Through sports, they learned teamwork, persistence, and how to manage both victory and defeat. More importantly, they knew I was always there, supporting them, playing with them, and showing them that no matter how busy life got, we'd always have time for each other.

Looking back, I realize that the time I've spent with my children, whether during a game of Uno or an intense backyard wrestling match, has been instrumental in their development. Fathers play such a vital role in shaping their children's sense of confidence, security, and self-worth. I've learned that being present and fully involved in their lives is one of the greatest gifts I could ever give them.

Play time wasn't just about having fun. It was about teaching them that they were important, that their father valued them, and that our time together mattered. Each game, each swing, each toss of the ball, was a way of communicating that I loved them deeply and without reservation.

Being active in my children's lives has helped them build physical strength and coordination, but it's also given them the emotional foundation they need to navigate the world. They've learned how to trust, how to interact with others, and how to set goals and work toward them. And as they've developed these skills, I've watched them grow into confident, caring individuals, capable of handling life's challenges with fortitude and grace.

What I love most about being a father is the time I get to spend with my children. Whether we're playing a game of catch or sitting together after a long day, those moments are the heartbeat of our relationship. I know that as they get older, these times will change, but the bond we've built through years of shared play and experiences will stay with them forever.

Something is enriching about seeing your children's faces light up when they accomplish something, like hitting a home run in baseball or building the tallest sandcastle in the backyard. And knowing that I played a part in helping them discover their potential is a feeling of accomplishment and pride that I will always treasure.

Being a father has never been about having all the answers or doing everything perfectly. It's always been about being present and willing to walk alongside your children as they grow. My kids may not remember every game of catch we played or every story I told, but they will remember that I was there, cheering them on from the sidelines, lifting them when they stumbled, and showing them through everyday moments what love looks like.

Our ordinary moments became extraordinary because they carried a message: you matter, and I'm here with you. Every investment of time shaped who they have become and what our relationship looks like into their adulthood. I've watched them grow into remarkable individuals, and I feel a deep sense of pride and gratitude. The journey was far from perfect, but it was rich, meaningful, and full of lessons for both them and me.

And truthfully, I wouldn't trade a single moment of it for the world.

CHAPTER
FIVE

The Emotional Anchor
Offering a Steady Hand

As fathers, we often imagine our role as protectors, providers, and mentors. But there is another equally important aspect of fatherhood that is often unspoken yet profoundly impactful: being the emotional anchor of the family. An emotional anchor is someone who provides stability and consistency, even when life becomes unpredictable or challenging. For a young father, this can feel like an immense responsibility. Yet it is one of the most powerful ways to create a safe and nurturing environment where your children feel understood and loved.

To be an emotional anchor doesn't mean you have to have all the answers or always appear stoic and unshakeable. Instead, it's about being a reliable presence, someone who listens and offers reassurance. As the emotional anchor, you set the tone for how your family handles feelings, whether in celebrating wins or working through challenges together. It's about providing the stability that allows each member of the family to be themselves and feel safe knowing they can turn to you for guidance and comfort.

One of the most valuable gifts you can give as an emotional anchor is your presence. This doesn't just mean being physically present but also fully engaged and mindful when you're with your family. Set aside distractions, put down the phone, and focus on being in the moment. Your children will feel your intentionality and sense that they are your priority, which helps build a stable bond and fosters trust. This emotional anchoring is never more vital than in moments when your child is facing a challenge that tests their limits, as I discovered during one high school football game.

It was a Friday night under the lights, the kind of night every high school football player dreams about. The crowd was buzzing, the band was playing, and I was sitting in the stands, my heart already swelling with pride. My son, Hayden, was playing outside linebacker, and though he wasn't the biggest guy on the field, he had a fire in him that he'd had since he was little.

The coaches asked him to do something no one else wanted to do that night: line up against the biggest lineman in the entire 4A division. Standing across from Hayden was a giant of a young man–6'5", 300 pounds–already committed to play for the Oregon Ducks after high school. Hayden, just 5'9" and 160 pounds, grinned at the challenge without hesitation. He wanted the opportunity.

From the very first snap, I could see the determination in him—Hayden was locked in. Play after play, I watched as he got knocked down, shoved aside, and thrown around like a rag doll. And yet, every single time, he picked himself up, clapped his hands, and lined up again. He never gave up. He didn't flinch or back down in the slightest. It wasn't about winning that one-on-one battle—it was about heart, courage, and refusing to quit.

Sitting there, I knew I had never seen so much determination in anyone in my whole life. It was one of those moments where a parent sees exactly who their child is deep down, and Hayden showed me that night he had the kind of grit that can't be taught. I realized something else in that moment: as his dad, I had the important role of being a steady anchor for my kids as they faced challenges bigger than themselves. Even as I watched my son go up against someone twice his size, I knew my presence in that moment—my support from the stands and my encouraging words after the game—would remind him he wasn't facing those challenges alone.

After the game, Hayden was glowing with excitement. He replayed each moment for my wife and me, his eyes bright as he said, "Can you believe I went against that guy?! He's going to play for Oregon!" He laughed, feeling the fresh bruises but already treasuring the experience. As he spoke, I looked at him with awe, so proud of his courage and the way he embraced a challenge no one else wanted. I hugged him tight and told him that I loved him and that he had played an amazing game. He smiled back and, with that same humble honesty that makes him who he is, said, "Yeah, but I got my butt kicked on almost every play."

We laughed, but in my heart, I knew what I had witnessed was bigger than a scoreboard or stats. It was a lesson in perseverance, in heart, and in the kind of character that makes me proud to be his dad every single day. And just as he found the strength to keep getting back up, I knew I'd always be there as his steady hand—his emotional anchor—through whatever challenges life put in front of him.

Being an emotional anchor doesn't only happen under the Friday night lights, but every day of the week. Consistently showing up for your kids builds confidence in your ability to always be a safe place for them. When you ask about their day, listen to their thoughts, and make time for simple moments like reading together, having family dinners, or just talking one-on-one, children are constantly reminded that you're there for them, providing a steady foundation on which they can rely.

Being an emotional anchor doesn't mean you have to hide your struggles or feelings. Showing vulnerability can amplify your role. By sharing, in appropriate age ways, when you're experiencing sadness or frustration, you teach your children that emotions are natural and that it's okay to talk about them.

For example, if you're facing a challenge at work or dealing with a stressful situation, acknowledging it and expressing how you plan to handle it can offer a valuable lesson. You're showing your children that even strong people experience ups and downs. Letting them see you handle adversity with patience, reflection, and kindness toward yourself shows them what healthy emotional processing looks like.

Emotional intelligence is a core part of being an emotional anchor. This means being aware of your own emotions, understanding others' emotions, and responding in a way that is empathetic and constructive. Developing these skills enables you to better handle family dynamics, work through conflicts, and offer guidance to your children.

As a young father, practice empathy by listening to your wife and children without judgment. When they're upset, actively listen rather than offering solutions. With your children, try asking questions to help them explore their feelings. Statements like, "How did that make you feel?" or "What do you think we should do next?" encourage them to reflect and develop self-awareness. Over time, these skills will help you become a trusted confidant and source of stability.

Being an anchor means holding steady to your values and consistently modeling them for your family. Kids learn by watching more than by hearing lectures, so embodying principles in your own life is vital. If you value hard work, let them see you work hard; if you value kindness, be kind to others in front of them. Over time, this consistency shows your children the importance of integrity and helps them feel secure knowing that they can count on you to stay true to your word.

Consistency also applies to discipline. Fairness, predictability, and setting clear expectations help children feel safe. When you discipline thoughtfully and calmly, you show them that while boundaries are important, they are enforced with love and respect.

As the emotional anchor, it's crucial to offer calmness during life's inevitable storms. Whether it's financial stress, family disagreements, or external crises, staying calm and composed helps reassure your family that everything will be okay. This doesn't mean pretending things are fine when they're not; it means addressing issues with a level head and working together to find solutions.

One way to cultivate calmness is by practicing stress management techniques like deep breathing, meditation, or simply taking time to decompress. When you model healthy ways of handling stress, you teach your children tenacity and self-care. Remember, they're watching and learning from how you respond to life's challenges.

While being an anchor is about providing support, it's also about knowing when to step back so your children can learn and grow. Encourage them to try new things, make decisions, and sometimes even make mistakes. Be there to catch them when they fall but resist the urge to solve every problem for them. When you allow them to navigate challenges independently, they develop self-confidence. Let them know you believe in their abilities and are there for guidance if they need it. This balance of support and independence helps them trust their own judgment while knowing they always have a safe place to return to.

My son Jackson shared a story that made me realize that being an emotional anchor encompasses more than I had ever imagined, and I was genuinely surprised by what he shared with me:

After high school, I was preparing to be a missionary for my church. My dad worked partly from home, and this was a huge blessing. I learned that I could rely on him for help because he was around a lot.

I left on my mission, but I was really struggling so I came home after about six months. I was so grateful that my dad was working from home during that time. I had lost a lot of confidence, but my dad helped me rebuild it. He encouraged me to keep moving forward and to stay productive. I really learned during that time that I could tell my dad anything. He never got mad and was grateful that I trusted him enough to share what I was going through.

When I moved to college, my dad started working close to where I was living. That was another huge blessing for me because during my first year of college, I had only one good friend and didn't really know my roommates. I knew I could call my dad for anything, and he told me he would drop whatever he was doing to help me if I needed it.

We started going to lunch once a week, and I could stop by his work whenever I needed to talk or ask for advice. I'm so glad he's close by and always willing to help with whatever he can. Having someone there for me in those critical moments built my confidence and reminded me that I'm never alone.

It was such a blessing for me to have the opportunity to be there for Jackson during that transitionary time in his life.

Each moment you spend listening, guiding, and simply being present is an investment in your child's emotional well-being and future. This role is a gift to your children and partner and a source of comfort that will be cherished for a lifetime.

The emotional safety you cultivate will influence your children's relationships, self-esteem, and how they approach life's challenges. By setting an example of consistency and empathy, you're helping your family build a foundation that will carry them through both the good times and the tough times. Being an anchor may feel like a heavy responsibility, but it is also one of the most rewarding parts of fatherhood.

When I became a father, I was a young man with a world of responsibilities that I hadn't fully anticipated. I was balancing a demanding job, trying to build a future, and figuring out who I was—all while taking on the role of a dad and husband. In those early years, I often felt stretched thin, struggling to be everything to everyone. But as time went on, I came to realize that my family needed something more than a provider; they needed someone they could lean on emotionally, someone who would be the constant in their lives no matter what else was happening. They needed an anchor.

One night, after a particularly challenging day at work, I came home to the usual scene of my wife amidst the kids' talking and laughter. As I took it all in, I decided it was time to do more than come home and just be there. I wanted to start a tradition that would allow us to connect more meaningfully as a family. So that night, I made tacos for dinner. As we ate, I talked to them about starting a new weekly tradition. I shared with them my "Ups and Downs of the Week" idea. It was a simple idea, but the kids lit up, and they took turns sharing their own "Ups and Downs." My wife and I joined in, too, and as I shared my high points and low points from the week, I realized how much this moment of vulnerability helped us connect. That night, we laughed and bonded in a way that felt different.

This little tradition quickly became the highlight of the week. Every Sunday, we cooked dinner and then we'd sit down to share our Ups and Downs. The kids started to look forward to it, saving up stories just so they'd have something to share on Sunday night. They loved hearing each other's "ups," celebrating the small victories, and they even loved comforting each other over the "downs," realizing that tough moments didn't have to be faced alone. I noticed a deeper connection forming between us, an openness that helped us navigate life's little struggles and joys together.

One Sunday evening, after we'd gone through our Ups and Downs, my son looked up at me and said, "Daddy, I love it when we do this; it's my favorite part of the week." That one sentence made every challenging day and long night worth it. It reminded me that being an anchor wasn't just about being strong during the hard times, it was about creating traditions, building memories, and being there in the small, everyday moments.

Over the years, our Sunday dinners became a cornerstone for our family. No matter what was going on in our lives, that time was sacred; it was a space where we could put everything else aside and just be together. It became a routine that grounded us, a constant reminder that no matter what else was going on in the world, we always had each other.

Being an anchor for your family isn't about having all the answers. It's about being someone they know they can count on. Through the simple act of sharing dinner and stories every week, I found my own way to be that anchor. In return, I gained a family tradition that keeps us connected, grounded, and grateful for each other every single day. Create your own routines and traditions to elevate your own family's emotional support system.

CHAPTER
SIX
The Role Model
Leading by Example

As role models, fathers guide their children through the challenging path of self-discovery, helping them to mold their values, beliefs, and behaviors. Yet, the role of a father is complex, and the impact of his presence—positive or negative—carries lasting consequences. The decisions a father makes, the way he treats others, and how he faces his struggles teach invaluable lessons, showing his children not only who he is but also who they can become.

From a young age, children look to their fathers as their first heroes and their first guides in life. A father's influence goes beyond words; it's in the gestures, the quiet examples, the routines, and the reactions to life's unexpected moments. Children absorb the way their father handles anger, celebrates success, comforts in sadness, and shoulders responsibility. His actions serve as a blueprint for understanding what it means to be a reliable friend, a loving partner, a dedicated worker, and a responsible individual. As children observe their father's approach to life, they start to form their own identities.

Research consistently reveals that a father's involvement in his child's life can lead to higher self-esteem, increased social skills, and a lower likelihood of risky behaviors. Fathers who are present, loving, and encouraging set a foundation that nurtures their child's mental, emotional, and social development. This connection often fosters a sense of security that children carry with them, allowing them to grow into confident individuals who trust in their worth and abilities.

The influence of a positive role model is transformative. Fathers who model high morals show their children the importance of living by positive values. These fathers don't just tell their children what is right; they live it out in front of them every day. A father who openly apologizes for mistakes, for instance, teaches his children that accountability is a strength, not a weakness. He shows them that taking responsibility builds trust and respect in relationships.

Engaging with his child's interests is another powerful way a father can model positive behavior. A father who sits with his child through soccer games, assists with science projects, or reads books together shows that their passions are worth celebrating. Such engagement doesn't only make the child feel valued, it bolsters their belief in pursuing their interests with curiosity and enthusiasm. By being invested in these small but meaningful moments, the father demonstrates the importance of dedication, encouraging his child to approach life with the same enthusiasm and determination.

Positive modeling also extends to how fathers handle conflicts and emotions. When children see their fathers communicate calmly in disagreement, listen attentively, and express their feelings constructively, they learn how to manage their own emotions. For instance, a father who empathizes with his child's struggles, patiently guiding them through, shows that love means being supportive and understanding. This teaches children that they can approach problems with resolve and that they are safe to feel and process their emotions.

However, a father's impact can also be a cautionary tale. When fathers display anger or aggression, children may internalize that as an acceptable way to handle stress. A father who uses harsh language or lashes out when upset teaches a lesson of his own—that anger is a force to wield against others, not a signal for self-reflection or communication. This model can plant seeds of fear or resentment, leaving children to navigate their own anger with confusion and possibly the same volatility.

Substance abuse or irresponsibility also leaves a lasting mark. A father who neglects family commitments due to unhealthy habits may unintentionally teach his child that such behavior is normal or acceptable. This absence of reliability shakes the foundation of trust, creating insecurities that can carry into adulthood. Children who witness this may struggle with commitment or even develop similar unhealthy coping mechanisms.

Disrespect toward others, especially within the home, is another detrimental example. A father who belittles or dismisses the opinions of others, especially those closest to him, sets a precedent. For instance, children who witness a father consistently disregard or insult their mother's contributions might adopt similar attitudes in their relationships. This kind of modeling skews a child's perception of respect and equality, leading to potential relational struggles in the future.

The influence fathers have on their children extends far beyond childhood. The lessons learned in a father's presence, both positive and negative, will be carried into future relationships, careers, and parenting styles. Children who grow up with fathers who model healthy behaviors are more likely to carry these behaviors into their own lives.

Negative examples, on the other hand, can leave children feeling unprepared for adult responsibilities or uncertain about their worth. For some, it may take years to unlearn unhealthy behaviors modeled for them. The impact of these patterns is often felt most acutely in relationships, where unresolved insecurities and attitudes learned from a father can resurface.

The beauty of fatherhood lies in the chance for continuous growth. Fathers have the opportunity to reflect on the behaviors and values they pass on. By seeking ways to improve and being open about their learning journey, fathers set an example of humility and growth. Those who identify negative behaviors in themselves can actively work to replace them with positive actions, thus reshaping the lessons they impart.

There's in seeking help, whether it's through therapy, support groups, or personal development books. A father who embraces self-improvement not only betters himself but also gives his children an inspiring role model who values growth. Children who see their father strive for betterment are more likely to do the same, understanding that life is a continuous journey of self-discovery and improvement.

Ultimately, the goal of fatherhood is to nurture children into well-rounded, capable, and compassionate adults. Fathers have the unique power to influence not only how their children see themselves but also how they see the world. By balancing love with accountability, guidance with freedom, and teaching with example, fathers offer their children a foundation of values and tools to face life with confidence.

My father was a towering figure of wisdom and kindness, has always been my role model. As a child, I was captivated by his intellect and problem-solving abilities. I'd watch in awe as he tackled household repairs, asking countless questions about the "whys" and "hows" of each step. His patience in explaining even the simplest concepts ignited a spark of curiosity within.

One summer, when I was about eight, my dad brought home a pile of sprinkler heads, valves, and pipes. I asked, "What is this?" and, "What are you going to do?" "You are going to install a sprinkler system," he announced. I was thrilled and immediately dove into the project, eager to prove my abilities. However, I quickly realized I was in over my head. I fumbled with the parts, unsure of where to start.

Instead of taking over, my father simply smiled. "Why don't you head to the library and see if you can find a book on sprinkler systems?" he suggested. So, I asked my mom to take me to the library to get a book on sprinkler systems, determined to figure it out. Hours later, I returned with a thick manual with lots of pictures, armed with newfound knowledge. With my father watching from a distance, I installed the sprinkler system feeling a sense of accomplishment I'd never experienced before.

The library became a place where I could explore my interests and satisfy my insatiable curiosity. Whether it was building model rockets, learning to fix my bike, or understanding the intricacies of the solar system, the library was always there to provide the answers I sought.

Beyond his technical skills, my father embodied a profound sense of service. I remember countless instances of him stopping to assist strangers in distress, whether it was changing a tire on a desolate highway or offering aid to a neighbor in need. His unwavering compassion and willingness to help without hesitation left an indelible mark on my heart.

Some of the most impactful lessons a father can teach come in the most unexpected moments—sometimes even in the middle of the night...

...It was a family trip to Costa Rica, and everyone was asleep in the house we were renting, when we were jolted awake by an awful smell. Groggy and confused, we soon realized that the bathroom had flooded with sewer water, spilling out and spreading across the floors. The smell was unbearable, and the sight was worse, as dark water seeped into every corner of the space where we had been sleeping. At that hour, with exhaustion heavy on us, it would have been easy to feel overwhelmed, maybe even angry. But I took a deep breath, got up, and quietly set to work mopping up the mess, focused only on containing the problem.

My son Jackson watched me, wide-eyed and unsure, and instead of retreating to his bed, he got up and joined me. Together, we grabbed towels and anything else we could find, mopping up the water and moving things to higher ground to keep them dry. As we worked, he didn't complain, and neither did I; we just focused on solving the problem, step by step. The whole situation could have soured our mood and could have put a dark mark on our vacation, but we stayed calm and got the job done.

Looking back, Jackson told me he remembers that night as a powerful lesson. He saw that even in the most unpleasant of situations, there's a choice: we can either let frustration take over, or we can simply handle the task at hand and keep moving forward. He learned that endurance means dealing calmly with life's unexpected messes, even when they sneak up in the middle of the night.

On that foreign night, soaked towels in hand, Jackson learned that even the worst setbacks don't have to ruin a good day or a good trip if we're willing to face them with patience and steadiness. Now, long after our Costa Rican adventure, he carries that lesson with him, a reminder that life's challenges can always be met with a helping hand and a bit of resolve—even when the floor is wet, the smell is awful, and everyone's tired.

Fathers teach through their actions and create a legacy, good or bad, that echoes through generations. Every moment spent modeling respect, showing compassion, and sharing in laughter becomes a cherished memory and an enduring lesson. Fatherhood is not just about being present today; it's about shaping a future filled with bravery, kindness, and the knowledge that love is the most lasting gift of all.

CHAPTER
SEVEN

The Support System
Fostering a Home of Love and Trust

When my daughter was only three-and-a-half years old, she decided she was done having training wheels on her bicycle. For months Natasha had pedaled happily with them attached, then one day she looked at me with determination and announced that those "dumb things" had to come off.

So I crouched beside her little bike, pulled the wheels away, and held onto the seat as she took her first wobbly rides up and down the road. My father stood nearby, cheering her on with his booming voice, while her great-grandmother smiled proudly from the van. I ran behind, out of breath and out of shape, trying to keep pace with her boundless energy.

And then it happened. Natasha reached back with her tiny hand, slapped my hand away, and insisted I let go. Pride and fear tangled inside me as I released my grip and watched her push forward. She leaned into her turns, nearly brushing against parked cars, but incredibly, she found her balance. At that moment, Natasha wasn't just a toddler on a bike—she was a little person tasting independence, testing her courage, and believing she could fly.

That picture has stayed with me after many years: three generations standing behind my precious daughter, cheering, guiding ... and letting go.

It's a beautiful example of what it means to nurture. Whether as parents, teachers, or mentors, our role is not only to hold steady when needed, but also to know when to step back and become the shadow at a child's side as they discover their own courage.

As we begin this chapter, I want to clarify that I understand that many families today look different from the traditional structure of father-mother-children, and that traditional roles are more fluid. In discussing what fathers and mothers contribute, feel free to substitute your own family's unique dynamics when thinking about who brings what to the table, and how you are creating your own support system that works for your family.

A family is more than just the people living under one roof; it's a unit built on shared experiences, values, and the support each person gives one another. At the heart of a traditional family system are fathers and mothers, whose roles, while sometimes similar, complement each other in unique ways. Together, they create a firm foundation that helps children learn and find their place in the world.

Parental roles can be distinct but united in one purpose: to nurture and guide their children into becoming compassionate and capable adults. The emotional support that parents provide is one of the most fundamental aspects of a family. Children need to feel safe and loved in order to thrive, and both mothers and fathers offer this in ways that shape a child's sense of self and security.

Traditionally, mothers take on the role of nurturers. They are usually the ones who comfort and reassure, who listen attentively, and provide immediate warmth and empathy when troubles arise. This kind of nurturing helps a child feel safe and understood, creating a solid base from which they can confidently explore the world.

Fathers often provide emotional support that teaches fortitude. They tend to encourage their children to face challenges head-on, to pick themselves up after a fall, and to see obstacles as opportunities to grow. Fathers often inspire children to take risks, try new things, and handle life's setbacks with courage.

For example, if a child falls while playing, a mother might comfort them, while a father might urge them to try again, teaching that picking yourself up and dusting yourself off is a part of life. And vice versa. This balance of nurturing and encouraging gives children the ability to feel secure yet adventurous, providing both emotional stability and the confidence to engage with the world around them.

Children learn a lot about life by watching their parents. In a family, role modeling plays a central part in teaching values and expected behaviors. Mothers often model traits like empathy, patience, and kindness. Through everyday interactions—whether it's showing patience in a busy household, resolving conflicts with understanding, or helping a friend in need—mothers demonstrate how to be caring and considerate. By witnessing these qualities, children learn the importance of empathy and kindness, gaining the skills they need to build respectful relationships.

Fathers might model assertiveness, problem-solving, and perseverance. They often showcase the importance of standing by one's principles, putting in hard work, and being honest. A father who commits to his job demonstrates to his children what it takes to support a family with consistency and determination.

In many families today, "traditional" roles are blended or swapped. This flexibility in parenting offers children a more nuanced understanding of human qualities and reminds them that both nurturing and providing are equally valuable in a support system, regardless of gender. Family life involves many responsibilities, from managing finances to keeping the household running smoothly. Both fathers and mothers play important roles in meeting these needs, though their contributions might differ based on individual skills and circumstances.

Traditionally, the mother has been the parent who manages daily routines and organizes schedules, meals, and other necessities. This attentiveness to detail keeps the household functioning and ensures that each family member's needs are met.

Fathers often contribute to the family's stability in different ways. They may handle financial planning, home repairs, or other long-term responsibilities, modeling reliability and a sense of duty. Through these contributions, fathers teach their children the importance of working toward future goals and maintaining a stable environment. For instance, a father might take on the role of teaching financial responsibility, discussing the importance of budgeting or saving for future needs. This approach reinforces the values of discipline and foresight, showing children how practical skills can support their goals.

Again, traditional roles as described are increasingly shared in today's families, with both parents contributing to household management and finances. This teamwork shows children that success in life often comes from collaboration and shared efforts, reinforcing values of cooperation and adaptability. Children who see their parents working together to maintain a stable, loving home learn that life's responsibilities are best managed when family members support one another.

Guiding children's personal growth is a central part of parenting, and both parents play active roles in this process. Mothers often focus on nurturing emotional intelligence and encouraging children to explore their passions. They might encourage children to express their feelings openly, validate their emotions, and explore interests like art, music, or sports. Through these supportive actions, mothers help children develop self-esteem and the courage to pursue their dreams.

Fathers often provide mentorship that focuses on practical skills and setting goals. They might teach children the importance of setting and working toward realistic aspirations and sharing insights from their own experiences. A father might discuss career paths, the value of education, and the importance of dedication and hard work. This kind of mentorship equips children to tackle real-world challenges with persistence and ambition.

Together, these different approaches allow children to explore their potential from every angle, balancing self-discovery with real-life preparedness. Children raised with this balanced guidance are not only more self-aware but also better equipped to achieve their goals.

Family values are the foundation of a healthy family unit. Mothers often act as the keepers of family traditions, preserving cultural practices, rituals, and family stories. Through shared traditions, they provide a sense of continuity and belonging, linking children to their heritage and extended family. A mother might share stories from her own childhood, teaching her children about the family's roots and reinforcing community support.

Fathers may emphasize the importance of character, honesty, and accountability. By modeling moral principles, fathers give their children a secure ethical foundation. When a father stands by his values in his own life, he shows his children the importance of living with integrity.

Modern parents work together to combine these traditional values with open-minded perspectives, teaching their children about equality and cultural understanding. By balancing traditional values with progressive ideas, parents prepare their children to thrive in a diverse and ever-changing world. Children raised with this blend of values learn respect for heritage while embracing the importance of adapting to new ideas.

When a family faces difficult times, the support of both parents is critical in helping children navigate these challenges. They can teach children that setbacks are part of life, using these moments to model adaptability. Together, mothers and fathers create a safety net that allows children to face life's ups and downs with courage, knowing that they have a family to rely on. This consistency provides reassurance, letting children know that they are loved and supported, even in uncertain times.

This unity teaches children that family is a source of support in both good times and bad. By witnessing their parents handling challenges together, children learn the value of cooperation and the power of having a united front.

Ultimately, the support and love both parents provide become the pillars of a child's life. By working together, fathers and mothers offer a gift that will shape their children's lives for years to come, creating memories and teaching values that they will carry forward into the next generation.

While talking to my son Hayden about writing this chapter, he had compelling stories from his youth to contribute. I will share his thoughts directly here:

"I don't remember every detail of the games I played or even all the final scores, but I do remember that both of my parents were always there. Every game, every tournament, no matter how small or how far, they showed up. And even if I didn't say it at the time, that simple act left a deeper mark on me than they probably knew.

Once during my sophomore year, my football team had an away game several hours away from home. I wasn't getting a lot of play time then, so I was mostly watching from the sidelines. But I remember looking into the stands and seeing my mom and dad there, all bundled up against the cold, and invested in the game like it was the championship. Just knowing they had made the drive and taken the time to be there for me meant everything. Seeing them there gave me a sense of purpose that made me want to push harder and prove myself.

The winter season brought wrestling tournaments. My parents knew I dreaded all of the early morning practices, the endless hours on the mat, and they also knew that I might only get to wrestle one or two matches. It felt like every other wrestler had an entire crowd cheering them on, but when it was my turn, the only two people there for me were my parents. But they were always there, and those two cheerleading voices grounded me in ways I could never really explain.

More than anything, my mom and dad taught me perseverance. Quitting was never an option in our house; I was raised not to walk away from something just because it was hard. My eighth-grade year of football tested that more than any other time. I played three snaps the entire season and felt like giving up every week. But Mom and Dad wouldn't let me quit. Even though I was frustrated and embarrassed, they told me to stick with it, to give it everything I had, and to push through no matter how tough it felt.

And because of that, everything changed. Over the next four years, I became a team captain, earned MVP three times, and developed a love for the game that shaped my life. They taught me that setbacks are just setbacks, and that giving up leaves a mark that sticks longer than any challenge.

Wrestling was a test, too. Sophomore year, I got sick with mono. I had to wrestle up a weight class and barely kept a .500 record. I complained every day, exhausted and ready to walk away. But my parents just listened, let me vent, and then reminded me, "You signed up for this." They wouldn't allow quitting, even when things felt impossible, and they showed me that finishing strong was about more than just sports, it was about sticking with something and proving that I could overcome anything that came my way.

Looking back, those lessons weren't just about football or wrestling; they shaped who I am. My parents taught me the importance of showing up no matter how tough things get. I carry those values with me every day, in everything I do. And I'll always carry the memory of my mom and dad in the stands, my most loyal supporters, reminding me of where I come from and what it takes not to quit.

When I hear my son talk about his experiences in our family support system growing up, one thing comes through loud and clear: It mattered that we were there. Not that we did everything perfectly, but that he knew we would always be there. You just have to keep showing up.

EIGHT

The Humble Man
Allowing Room for Imperfection

When a man becomes a father, he steps into a role filled with responsibilities and expectations he may have never anticipated. Whether he's cradling his newborn for the first time, trying to console a teething toddler, or guiding a teenager through life's complexities, he often finds himself wondering if he's doing enough or doing it right. Like many other men, he probably envisioned fatherhood as a place where he'd be the steady rock—always wise, strong, and prepared. It is humbling for a man to realize that fatherhood can be a long journey filled with uncertainty and anxiety. The good news is it is also a profoundly rewarding journey if he can learn to embrace the discomfort of not having all the answers.

As fathers, we're often given subtle (or not-so-subtle) messages about what it means to be a "good" dad. Society can broadcast an image of a perfect dad as a man who works hard, is emotionally present, always makes time for family, never loses his patience, and knows exactly how to fix every problem that arises. But the reality is quite different. Real fatherhood is filled with moments that challenge patience, moments of feeling unsure, and moments when a father wonders if he's missed the mark entirely. Embracing imperfection helps a man realize that these moments are not failures but normal experiences most men have in fatherhood.

Accepting one's imperfections as a father can begin with small acts of vulnerability—like admitting we don't have all the answers when we make mistakes or feel overwhelmed. It's liberating to acknowledge that perfection isn't the goal, and that growth comes from learning alongside our children. This shift isn't always easy. For many fathers, vulnerability feels counterintuitive, especially if they've been raised with ideals of toughness or emotional restraint. But fatherhood has a unique way of bringing vulnerability to the surface, often showing that, sometimes, the strongest thing we can do is admit we don't have it all together.

In parenthood, as in life, mistakes are inevitable. There will be times when words come out sharper than intended, or when stress from work spills over into family life. Perhaps a father misses an important event because of obligations or says "no" to something he later regrets. These moments can feel heavy, especially when they happen in front of those we love. But instead of letting these moments weigh them down, fathers can see them as opportunities to learn and grow.

One of the greatest gifts a father can give his children is the example of humility—the ability to say, "I was wrong," or "I'm sorry." It's in these apologies and honest moments that children learn it's okay to be human. They see firsthand that mistakes are part of life, but that what matters is how we handle them. Rather than feeling burdened by imperfection, fathers can use these experiences to show their children that growth comes from facing our mistakes and doing what we can to correct them. This model of accountability becomes a powerful lesson in humility, showing children that we can learn from our missteps and even make our relationships stronger when our mistakes are handled with love and grace.

Fatherhood is a constant balancing act. Every stage of a child's life presents new, unfamiliar challenges. A father of a toddler may struggle to understand their frustration, just as a father of a teenager grapples with issues like independence, peer pressure, or finding the right balance between discipline and freedom. No handbook can prepare a father for every situation; we simply do the best we can and try to embrace imperfection.

Humble fathers learn to face each new challenge with an open mind, recognizing that finding solutions is usually a process of trial and error. Each day, fathers are given the chance to try, reflect, and grow, knowing that while they may not have it all figured out, it's okay because they are leading with love.

For many fathers, success can feel like a moving target. They may set expectations for themselves based on how they were raised or what they see around them, often aiming for ideals that are hard to reach. But in embracing imperfection, fathers have the chance to redefine what success looks like in a way that reflects their family's unique journey. Success for your family can be measured by whether or not you were present, listen well, and exhibit unconditional love. A successful father supports and uplifts his family at all times. This perspective allows fathers to see themselves not as failures when they fall short, but as role models who are doing their best, and who are willing to learn from each step of the journey.

Embracing imperfection in fatherhood also opens the door to appreciating the small, everyday victories that might otherwise go unnoticed. It's easy to get caught up in the pressures of being a "perfect" dad, so much so that we forget to appreciate the joy in smaller, quieter moments—like when a father sees his child's face light up as he reads them a bedtime story, or when they share a laugh after a long day.

These small moments may not seem monumental, but they are the heart of fatherhood. They remind fathers that love is found not in grand gestures, but in the small, steady acts of presence, gentleness, and unwavering support. Each moment of connection becomes a reminder that they don't need to be perfect to make a positive, lasting impact. Fathers who allow themselves to celebrate these small victories find joy in every day, knowing that fatherhood isn't a destination, but a journey filled with countless meaningful moments along the way.

A father who embraces his imperfections becomes a powerful teacher. He shows his children that life isn't about having all the answers, but about being willing to grow and adapt. By default, these experiences actually demonstrate to children that it takes a big person to admit when they're wrong and try to make it right. They see that true strength lies not in never faltering, but in continuing to show up, learn, and grow. When children see their father embracing his humanity, they learn to embrace their own. They understand that mistakes are not failures but stepping stones toward self-discovery. This kind of role modeling gives children the courage to be themselves, to take risks, and to live life fully, knowing that they are enough even when they make mistakes.

Fatherhood is a lifelong journey, one that doesn't end when children reach adulthood. Humble fathers always grow alongside their children, finding new ways to connect and support them even as they become adults. Embracing imperfection in fatherhood is a gift for fathers and their families. It's a journey of self-acceptance that brings greater joy, connection, and understanding. It allows fathers to live fully in each moment, to love without reservation, and to model the kind of compassion and resilience that will echo through generations. Humble fathers guide their children with a fully open, imperfect, and endlessly loving heart.

I have many stories I could share about how I learned from my mistakes as a dad, but one in particular comes to mind...

It was one of those days when everything started with the best of intentions. My son and I were working on a project together. I thought it would be a great chance to bond, teach, and accomplish something with him. But as we got deeper into the task, frustration started to creep in. I had a very clear vision of how the project should go, the steps we needed to take, and how the finished product would look. In my mind, I was doing it the right way—I was being efficient and dependable.

My son, however, had other ideas. He was tackling the project differently in a way that felt completely wrong to me. At first I tried to explain and to steer him toward my plan, but he wasn't listening. Or at least, that's how it felt. Every time I gave directions, my son pushed back with his own thoughts. My patience wore thin. The more I insisted, the more determined he seemed to do it his way.

Eventually, I hit my breaking point. I got upset, frustrated, and angry. "Why can't he just listen to me?!" I thought as I walked away, muttering to myself. I was upset that things weren't being done how I envisioned. After all, I had more experience, didn't I? I knew what I was doing, and this project *needed* to be done the right way.

After a little while, my wife gently pulled me aside. She'd seen the whole thing play out and, in her calm, knowing way, said something that stopped me in my tracks: "Listen to his idea. Let him try it his way. If it doesn't work, he'll learn. But he deserves the chance to try."

Her words sank deeper than I wanted to admit. I realized I wasn't just upset about the project; I was holding onto control, afraid to let him make mistakes or go on a different route. Maybe he *would* fail, but my wife was right, that's how you learn. And maybe, just maybe, I was wrong.

I took a breath and went back to find my son. I sat down next to him and said, "Hey, I'm sorry for earlier. I got frustrated, but I want to hear your ideas. Show me what you're thinking."

My son's face lit up with that mix of surprise and pride that only a kid can express. He explained his idea step by step, and even though I still had doubts, I told him I supported him. "Let's do it your way," I said.

We got back to work, this time with me helping him instead of fighting him. I watched as his plan unfolded, and to my surprise, it started to come together...quickly. By the time we finished, I had to step back and take it all in. Not only did his way work, but it turned out to be *faster* and *better* than what I had envisioned.

I looked at him and couldn't help but laugh at myself. "You know what, buddy? I was wrong," I admitted. "Your way was more efficient than what I was going to do. Thank you for showing me that."

He beamed proud not only of his work, but of the trust I'd given him. At that moment, I realized that listening to him, supporting his ideas, and giving him space to try was far more valuable than getting the project done my way.

I had thought our father-son task was just a building project, but it turned out to be so much more. I learned that day that if I let go of my pride, I could let my son learn and grow on his own—that I could be a trusted guide who respects his ideas and leads with love. Those were invaluable lessons that I will never forget.

CHAPTER
NINE

Leaving A Legacy
The Everlasting Impact of Dad

My son Jackson had a fascination with tractors when he was three years old. He spent hours in the sandbox with his toy backhoes and diggers, carefully carving roads and trenches in the dirt as if he were building something grand. It was no surprise, then, that when he got the chance to sit on the real thing—Grandpa's 580K Spacko backhoe—he was excited beyond words.

Grandpa sat Jackson with him on the big machine and they started digging a trench for an irrigation line alongside my house. Jackson's small hands rested gently on top of my dad's strong, weathered ones as they worked the controls together. At first, he was just following along, soaking in the feel of the machine's power and rhythm through his grandfather's steady guidance.

But it didn't take long before my son's determination came through. With the same confidence he had in the sandbox, Jackson started pushing my dad's hands away from the levers, insisting he was ready to do it on his own.

Then my dad did something unexpected—he let my little boy take over.

My father sat back, staying close, ready to steady the machine if needed, but he gave Jackson the space to lead. To my surprise (and slight panic), Jackson was soon working the controls himself, lowering the bucket into the ground, scooping dirt, and carving out that trench. Every time the backhoe shook or the angle grew tricky, my dad would step in just enough to keep things safe, but never enough to take away Jackson's sense of control.

I stood there watching, my heart racing. We were right next to the side of my house, and all I could think of was what could go wrong. But my dad's calm presence and confidence in Jackson forced me to pause. He trusted my son's ability, even at three years old, to rise to the moment. And if he could trust him, then so could I.

Jackson didn't just dig a trench that day; he lived out a dream that began in his sandbox. In that moment, I saw humility at work across three generations—my dad's humble trust in his grandson, my son's humble courage to try, and my own humbling reminder that fatherhood often means stepping back so they can step forward. Fatherhood isn't always about holding tight, but bravely letting go.

I had to let go of my father on a quiet Sunday. It was a reminder of how fragile the balance of life truly is. I was not ready to let him go, and I doubt anyone who knew him would have been. He embodied a rare combination of strength and gentleness, a steady presence marked by compassion, and an unwavering devotion to family and friends.

He was more than my father, he was my companion, my guide, and often my sounding board. He offered wisdom without force, allowing me the space to make my own choices, even my mistakes, while remaining close enough to steady me when I faltered. From him I learned what it means to be both a good man and a good father—lessons taught not through grand speeches but through a life quietly and consistently lived.

Perhaps what I cherish most is knowing that my children had time with him, that they were able to see for themselves the qualities I had long admired. His influence does not end with his passing. It endures in the values he instilled, in the stories we carry, and in the way his children and grandchildren continue forward with pieces of his love woven into their lives. In that way, his presence remains, even in absence.

Fathers are often our first heroes. They are the figures who shape our earliest ideas about morals and values. From the moment we're born, our fathers stand as guiding lights, helping us understand the world around us. Whether through grand gestures or quiet, everyday actions, dads fill our lives with memories and lessons that slowly shape who we are. They create a foundation of support that becomes our springboard into life. Fathers make us feel safe enough to explore, brave enough to try, and secure enough to dream. From them, we learn the first truths about navigating life's challenges and celebrating its joys.

For many of us, our earliest memories involve our fathers teaching us something valuable. Perhaps they were the ones who helped us learn how to ride a bike, patiently guiding us until we could pedal on our own. Maybe they were the ones who took us outside on clear nights, pointing out stars and telling us stories about the universe. Or they might have simply been the constant, reliable figure, always there to listen or offer advice. Each of these moments, while sometimes taken for granted, forms a powerful bond that grows with time. The memories of these simple acts of guidance stick with us, quietly shaping how we view the world and our place within it.

Fathers influence their children's lives in both big and small ways, leaving impressions that can last a lifetime. They don't need grand gestures to teach us important lessons; often, it's the little things they do that carry the most weight. Dads teach us to keep going when we fall and to celebrate the small victories along the way. They remind us that persistence matters and that giving our best effort is something to be proud of. These early lessons become more than childhood memories; they're the building blocks of a child's self-worth.

Dads prepare us for the world, and they do so in ways that allow us to feel both safe and capable. They are often our first examples of perseverance, empathy, and integrity, showing us through actions what it means to be strong and kind. Whether or not they openly express their love, fathers show it in the way they're there for us, modeling qualities that shape us far more than words could. Many dads lead by example, knowing that it's not just what they say but what they do that matters most. Their actions—big or small, frequent or rare—create a silent guide that stays with us even after we're grown and far from home.

Fathers help us build a solid foundation and a sense of who we are and what we can achieve. As our first heroes, they provide us with more than just guidance; they give us a template for facing the world with courage and compassion. The impact they have may not always be seen or spoken about, but it's felt deeply and remembered for a lifetime. Through their presence, fathers leave a lasting mark on our lives, a mark that continues to influence us as we grow, shaping our values, our actions, and ultimately, the people we become.

In a society where masculinity is often linked to being tough or emotionless, fathers navigate a balance between strength and vulnerability, redefining what it means to be a strong man. Traditionally, fathers were seen mostly as providers or protectors, yet today, many fathers recognize the value of emotional openness with their children. This shift allows them to be human, with all their imperfections, fears, and hopes. When fathers allow themselves to be seen this way, they send a powerful message: it's okay to be fully human. By embracing both strength and vulnerability, dads empower their children to do the same.

A father who openly admits mistakes and doesn't shy away from expressing love or emotion is showing his children that vulnerability is not weakness. This approach teaches children the power found in honesty and connection. Fathers demonstrate this by being authentic and by sharing their own stories of trials and triumphs—allowing their children to see both their strong and weak sides. These moments provide a lifelong blueprint for how to handle life's ups and downs.

Fathers' examples often resonate beyond specific lessons. Their everyday acts of patience, dedication, and empathy teach children about being reliable and kind, even when times are hard. Fathers show that power is present in both big moments and small ones, like staying calm in a crisis or simply listening without judgment. Their willingness to show up for others and to extend kindness even when it's difficult becomes a model for navigating relationships. Fathers don't always have the answers, and they don't need to; their presence, even in uncertain times, builds a sense of trust that lasts a lifetime.

A dad's commitment to being present is one of his greatest gifts. The legacy of a father's strength and vulnerability is measured by his authenticity, not his perfection. Children carry these lessons with them throughout life, using them as guiding principles that help them feel capable and connected to others. This enduring influence becomes a part of who they are, shaping their values and interactions long after childhood is over.

Fathers frequently put aside their dreams, comforts, and time so their children have the chance for a better life. These sacrifices might not always be dramatic or visible; they happen quietly. It might be a father who works late nights or weekends, forgoing personal time to provide. Perhaps it's a dad who puts off his aspirations to focus on his child's education or opportunities. These sacrifices, although understated, make a deep and lasting impact on a child's life.

It usually takes time for children to understand the full extent of their father's sacrifices. As children grow up, they may begin to realize that their dad's absence at home or his focus on work wasn't indifference, but a choice driven by love and responsibility. The realization of these unseen sacrifices can build deep respect and gratitude for fathers, shaping how children view dedication and hard work. Fathers who quietly go out of their way to provide a better life for their families teach their children about selflessness and the power of love in action.

Dads don't usually seek recognition for their sacrifices; instead, they take pride in their children's success and happiness. This quiet selflessness forms the cornerstone of a father's legacy, a gift of commitment that speaks louder than words. A father's sacrifices become lessons in what it means to be selfless and dedicated, a living example of love that reaches beyond words. This legacy of commitment and love goes beyond any material provision; it becomes a part of the child's character, instilling values that shape how they live and what they believe is important.

The impact of a father's sacrifices is profound, creating a foundation of love and support that resonates through generations. Fathers remind us that love often means putting others first and that real happiness comes from seeing those we care about thrive. In teaching their children selflessness through actions, fathers leave behind a legacy that's impossible to measure but always deeply felt.

As children grow, their relationship with their fathers often transforms. What begins as a relationship of authority gradually turns into one of friendship, mutual respect, and understanding. Fathers impart lessons early on, but as their children experience the world for themselves, these lessons take on new meaning. Simple advice like "always do your best" resonates differently when children face their obstacles, realizing how much their father's words of encouragement help keep them grounded.

In adulthood, a father's influence becomes even clearer, showing up in the decisions his children make, the values they hold, and the way they treat others. Fathers often teach us to stand tall, to trust in ourselves, and to approach life with respect and kindness. These lessons, sometimes learned through struggle or challenge, become invaluable gifts that last a lifetime. Fathers encourage us to face adversity with bravery, work for what matters, and see humor even in tough times.

A father's influence doesn't end with his children; it often extends to how they parent or mentor others.

Fathers pass on more than physical traits; they pass down an entire worldview, shaping not only their children but also future generations. Through fathers, we learn the importance of tradition, values, and the need to carry forward love into each new generation. This living legacy is woven through generations, influencing how each one approaches life, love, and family.

A father's love, even when not spoken, is one of the most powerful forces in life. It shapes us, expands us, and helps us become the best versions of ourselves. The everlasting impact of dads isn't just in what they do but in who they are—a constant, loving presence that teaches us to be strong, compassionate, and true. This legacy of love and wisdom extends far beyond a single lifetime, shaping us and the generations to come. We do not realize the everlasting impact dads have on their children.

Even after fathers are no longer physically present, their influence endures, like a quiet, guiding presence. We feel it in our choices, in our memories, and in the strength we summon during tough times. A father's impact is more than physical—it becomes a part of how we see ourselves and the world. When fathers pass on, their love, lessons, and sacrifices remain within us, shaping us as we continue forward.

The following is my son Hayden's thoughts on the lasting impact of dads:

I served as a religious missionary in Alaska when I was 19 years old. Everything started fine—it was challenging, yes, but it was manageable. About six months in, winter arrived. We were so close to the North Pole that we hardly had any sunlight, and I started feeling trapped in the dark, both inside and out. I was hit hard with seasonal depression and began to question my purpose there. Week after week, I'd FaceTime my parents, looking for help to endure the endless nights.

Never once did my dad try to "toughen me up" or tell me stories about how his own mission was just as hard. Instead, he just listened and reminded me of my purpose: to truly convert myself to Christ and help others experience the same. His reassuring words pulled at my core, grounding me in the mission I'd set out to accomplish.

Then, just when I thought I'd weathered the hardest part, COVID-19 swept through. Quarantine isolation grew intense, and every part of the mission felt like it had come to a halt. I thought about leaving, as did many others. I had people telling me it was okay to go, that quitting might even be the right decision. But my parents reminded me once again of my purpose and told me that everything in life is an opportunity. My dad encouraged me to use the time to study and to deepen my knowledge of the Savior. It was in those weeks that my foundation of faith took on a depth it hadn't had before. I truly learned what it meant to hold steady, to keep going, and to trust. Not quitting became one of the defining experiences of my life, and I have my dad to thank for that.

Those were just two recent years in a lifetime of lessons I learned from my dad. Some of the most important values I learned from him are dependability and integrity. From as early as I can remember, I watched my dad live out principles like these in our everyday life. We spent many weekends helping people move, joining service projects, setting up flags on holidays, or taking our turn to clean the church building. Any time Dad said he would do something, he did it. He taught, "Your word is your honor," and he lived that truth, no matter how inconvenient it might have been. That has stuck with me.

I followed my dad everywhere as a kid, sometimes right underfoot. There were times he'd turn around and nearly trip over me because I was so close behind. When I learned to talk, the questions started. I wanted to know why he did things a certain way, or how something worked. At first, Dad would get frustrated, probably thinking I was challenging him, but once he realized that I was genuinely curious, he always took the time to explain things. I may have taught him some patience, but he taught me that it's okay not to know everything and that asking questions is part of learning.

From the time I could hold a shovel, my dad had my brother and me outside working in the yard. I dreaded it for a while, and even now, when he mentions a new project, there are moments I'd rather skip out. But shovel by shovel, wheelbarrow by wheelbarrow, he taught me the value of hard work. He also showed me what it meant to be resourceful.

I'll never forget the day we helped Uncle David lay sod in his yard. There were about 20 people there, but as I looked around, I realized that the ones doing the heavy lifting were my dad, my younger brother, and me. While others stood around, we worked hard, side by side. Seeing us pull through as a team made me proud to be my dad's son. I realized that not only had he taught us the skills for landscaping, but he'd instilled in us the principles of hard work and service.

The values I learned from my dad—values like integrity, dependability, patience, and hard work—are at the core of who I am. These lessons didn't just come from his words, but from watching him demonstrate them in practice, day in and day out. From our talks during the dark days of my mission to the countless projects we tackled together, my dad shaped me in ways I couldn't fully understand until now. He showed me the strength it takes to be a man of faith, to honor my word, and to stand tall, even when it would be easier to quit. And in those values, I carry his legacy forward.

Dads in particular have a huge impact on who their sons become. When a father looks back to the relationship he had with his own dad as a kid, he sees the effect his dad had on him, for better or worse. Fathers shouldn't just give advice; they should live by example. They should show us what it looks like to keep our word, to push through, and to believe in something bigger than ourselves. We watch our fathers and carry everything we learned from them forward into the rest of our lives.

CHAPTER
TEN
Building a Strong Foundation for Future Generations

Fathers hold a unique and powerful role in shaping future generations. They are examples through their words and actions. Reflecting on my own father's influence, I see how his leadership and love created a solid foundation for me to step into fatherhood with confidence and purpose. His lessons, often subtle but profound, taught me values that I now strive to pass on to my children. In this way, fathers are architects of legacy, building structures of integrity and respect that can be passed down through generations.

I learned from my father that respect was non-negotiable. It wasn't something he lectured about; it was something he lived. Whether it was greeting a neighbor with a kind word, holding the door open for a stranger, or speaking to us with calm authority even when we pushed his limits, he showed me that respect begins with how you treat others.

One summer when I was about 10 years old, Dad gave me the job of mowing our elderly neighbor's lawn. I grumbled. It was hot and boring, and I'd much rather be riding my dirt bike. But Dad didn't budge. "This isn't just about the lawn," he said, "It's about helping someone who needs it and doing the right thing without being asked." Over time, I came to understand what he meant, and I found pride in the work. That lesson stayed with me—respect isn't just about words; it's about action. He instilled in me the value of being helpful.

My dad had a way of turning every chore into a teaching moment, even if I didn't realize it at the time. We always raked leaves in the fall, and we always seemed to be painting, painting, painting! He taught me not just how to do a job, but why it mattered. He would say things like, "Every small effort adds up," and, "When you pitch in, you make things better for everyone."

One winter, we spent hours shoveling snow from our driveway and the sidewalks for the entire block. As we worked, I remember asking my dad why we couldn't just stop at our property line. He smiled and said, "Because it's not just about us. It's about the kind of community we want to live in." That day, he taught me about community responsibility and the ripple effect of small acts of kindness.

Patience was another cornerstone of my dad's teachings, though I'll admit it was a harder lesson for me to learn. As a child, I had a habit of rushing through tasks, eager to finish so I could move on to something more fun. But Dad never let me take shortcuts. If I swept the garage and missed a corner, he'd hand me the broom and have me start again. "If you're going to do something," he'd say, "do it right the first time." There were times when I'd get frustrated, but he never lost his cool. Instead, he'd take the time to show me the right way to do things, even if it meant the job took twice as long.

Looking back, those moments weren't just about teaching me to be thorough, they were about teaching me the value of persistence and the satisfaction of a job well done. My father's leadership extended beyond chores and daily responsibilities. He led by example in every aspect of his life.

When I was 12 years old, I wasn't exactly the most diligent worker. Sure, I could get a job done, but often my "best" wasn't exactly up to adult standards. I learned this the hard way one summer afternoon when my uncle asked me to help clean a construction site of apartments that my dad was building on 14th Street. I thought it would be an easy task—sweep a little here, pick up some trash there, and maybe grab a soda in between. But what started as a simple chore turned into a lesson in responsibility and respect, all wrapped in a story that still makes me laugh and cringe in equal measure.

So it began with my uncle assigning me cleaning duties at the construction site. The job wasn't anything monumental, sweeping sawdust, gathering scraps, and keeping the area tidy. Simple enough, right? Except, at age 12, I didn't have much pride in my work, and it showed. I'd sweep a section only to have my uncle point out all the corners I'd missed and demand I do it again. He wasn't wrong, but that didn't stop me from feeling frustrated. With every critique, my irritation grew, and it wasn't long before I decided I'd had enough.

After one particularly heated scolding, I grabbed my things and left the site. I didn't tell my uncle and didn't make a big scene; I just walked off. In my mind, I was staging a grand protest. In reality, I was a kid walking down the street in a pair of football cleats, blistering my heels with every step. My house was a good 15 miles away, but I didn't care. I was determined to leave that job behind, even if it meant limping all the way home.

I made it about five blocks before my resolve began to waver. The sun was hot and my feet were killing me. The cleats were starting to feel like instruments of torture. That's when I saw it: the Flying J gas station, a beacon of air conditioning and a payphone. I hobbled inside, dropped a quarter into the phone, and called the one person I knew would take my side: Mom.

The phone barely rang before she picked up. "Mom," I said, trying to sound as pitiful as possible, "Uncle is being so mean. He keeps making me redo everything, and he's asking me to do way more than I was supposed to. Can you come get me?"

I waited, expecting her to leap into action, ready to swoop in and rescue her poor baby boy. "Okay," she said, "I'll be right there." Relief washed over me. I'd won! I'd outsmarted my uncle and escaped the nightmare of cleaning those apartments. Or so I thought...

About 20 minutes later, a car pulled into the Flying J parking lot, but it wasn't my mom behind the wheel—it was my dad. My heart sank. I should've known better. My dad was the type of man who believed in finishing what you started, no matter how unpleasant the task.

Dad didn't say much as I climbed into the car, my cleats squeaking against the floor mat. We drove back to the construction site in silence, the only sound was the hum of the engine and the rhythm of Dad's fingers drumming the steering wheel.

When we pulled up, my dad finally spoke. "You're going to finish the job," he said firmly, "But first, we're going to set some expectations."

Over the next few minutes, my dad calmly laid out what he expected from me: work hard, take pride in what I was doing, and stick it out until the job was done. Then he turned to my uncle and set some boundaries for him, too, explaining that while I needed to be held accountable, I was still just a kid and not an adult employee.

With that, my dad left, and I went back to work. I'd like to say I dove in with newfound enthusiasm, but the truth is, I grumbled through most of it. Still, my dad's words stuck with me. He hadn't sided with me, but he hadn't completely sided with my uncle either. Instead, he'd taken a middle road that balanced responsibility with fairness, teaching me a lesson I didn't fully appreciate at the time.

Looking back, that day was a turning point for me. Yes, I learned the importance of finishing a job, but I also learned to take ownership of my actions and understand the importance of doing things right, even when it's hard or frustrating. My dad could've easily let me quit and chalked it up to me being a kid, but he didn't. He saw an opportunity to teach me something bigger than sweeping floors.

While my dad may not have been the hero I wanted that day, he was exactly the hero I needed.

And those football cleats? They were the perfect metaphor for the experience—uncomfortable and unforgiving, but ultimately a tool that helped me move forward. Even now, when I'm faced with a tough task or a moment where quitting feels like the easier option, I think back to that long walk from 14th Street. It reminds me that responsibility isn't always convenient, but it is always worth it.

Now, as a father myself, I often find myself wishing I could emulate the same balance my dad showed that day. I hope to teach my children the importance of hard work, respect, and accountability while still being compassionate enough to understand their limits. I want to be the kind of father who doesn't just bail them out but equips them with the tools and lessons they need to succeed.

When I think about the kind of father I want to be, I often find myself wishing I could emulate more of my dad's qualities. I am glad to have his patience when my children test the limits. I showed them the same unwavering respect that he showed me, even when I didn't always deserve it. I wish to create moments of learning and growth just as he did for me so that my children grow up understanding the values of respect, helpfulness, and patience. Most of all, I wish to lead my children with the same love and compassion that defined my father's every action.

I would like to think that the foundation my father built for me is one I am continuing to build for my children. His influence has shaped how I approach fatherhood; from the way I handle challenges to the way I celebrate small victories. He showed me that being a father isn't about perfection; it's about presence. Through his leadership, love, and compassion, my dad didn't just teach me how to be a good man; he showed me how to build a legacy that will last for generations.

CHAPTER
ELEVEN
Reflecting on the Journey of Fatherhood

The journey of fatherhood begins with a mixture of awe and uncertainty. Holding his baby for the first time, a new dad's world feels both bigger and smaller. In that instant, many fathers find themselves face to face with the weight of love and responsibility, knowing they'll do anything to protect their child. With that first touch, there's a shift—a realization that life will never be the same. The journey of fatherhood is one that's filled with growth to become someone that a little person will look up to. It is an experience of vulnerability and love in ways that are new and profound.

In the early days of parenthood, there is a steep learning curve. Fathers and mothers find themselves navigating sleepless nights, endless diaper changes, and the delicate art of soothing a crying baby. With nights spent holding their child, humming softly until tiny eyes close, a parent begins to discover depths of patience they never knew they had.

They learn the language of parenthood through trial and error, adapting to this new role. Little by little, they grow in confidence, realizing that the bond they're building goes beyond words. Every touch, every gentle rocking, and every lullaby creates a foundation of trust and love.

These initial moments of fatherhood are humbling. It's in these moments of humility and wonder that a father's journey truly begins. The first steps into fatherhood may be filled with uncertainties, but they're also marked by a newfound, quiet, enduring commitment to showing up and doing the best they can for their child.

As children grow, so do their fathers. The early milestones— first steps, first words, first smiles—fill fathers with pride and awe, reminding them of the magic in life's simplest moments. Each milestone is a reminder of the rapid pace of time, and fathers begin to cherish every little thing. They realize they are not just caretakers; they are teachers, guides, and playmates. They are learning alongside their children, gaining patience, compassion, and a sense of wonder through their children's eyes.

With each scraped knee, missed baseball catch, or frustrated school day, fathers find themselves in the role of comforter, encouraging their children to persevere. They teach through gentle words and supportive actions, helping their children find confidence in the face of life's small struggles. Fathers soon realize that rather than shielding their children from hardship, they can stand nearby in support as children learn to navigate trials. They become a steady presence, one that reminds their children they're never alone, no matter what life brings.

In these shared moments of growth, fathers gain something invaluable—the perspective that parenting is less about control and more about guidance. They learn that their role isn't to mold their child into someone they envision but to support them as they discover who they are. This realization deepens the bond, allowing fathers to connect with their children on a more profound level. By growing together, fathers and children create a relationship built on mutual respect, trust, and love.

Fatherhood is filled with lessons that shape not only the children but the fathers themselves. Dads see their strengths and weaknesses reflected in their children's eyes, teaching them to confront and embrace their humanity. Every mistake becomes a lesson in humility, and every success a reminder of the privilege of guiding a young life. Fathers come to understand that they are still students of life just as much as their children are.

As we've established many times in this book, one of the greatest lessons fatherhood imparts is the importance of presence. The realization that quality time matters more than material possessions or grand gestures shapes how fathers spend their days. Simple moments—reading bedtime stories, building LEGO towers, or tossing a baseball—become cherished rituals and lifetime memories. Fathers understand that these are the times their children will remember most, the moments that will shape their children's memories of love and family. The act of showing up, day in and day out, becomes the most profound way of saying, "I love you."

Fathers also learn the power of forgiveness—both in giving and receiving it. They come to terms with their imperfections, understanding that mistakes are part of the journey. When they apologize to their children or forgive themselves for a misstep, they're teaching a valuable lesson: that love means embracing flaws and choosing connection over pride. Fatherhood teaches them that they are allowed to be human, and in doing so, they show their children how to accept their humanity.

Fatherhood brings boundless joy, but it's also filled with challenges. There are moments of frustration, of worry, of self-doubt. Fathers often find themselves balancing the demands of work, personal goals, and family life, a juggling act that isn't always easy. They face the weight of responsibility and the silent pressure to be a source of stability and security for their family. Yet, in these challenges, fathers discover their inner strength. Each struggle they face becomes a testament to their commitment, a reminder of the depth of their love.

The joys of fatherhood come in countless forms: the laughter shared over silly jokes, the pride in seeing a child achieve something they worked hard for, and the simple warmth of a hug. These moments make the hard days worth it, reminding fathers why they embarked on this journey in the first place. Even the smallest joys—a spontaneous "I love you," or a quiet moment watching their child sleep—are enough to bring a sense of peace and fulfillment that's hard to describe. Fatherhood, despite its challenges, is a journey filled with priceless, irreplaceable rewards.

In facing both the highs and lows, fathers learn the importance of balance. They realize that strength comes from rising every time you falter. They learn to prioritize what truly matters, finding a way to give their best to their families without losing themselves in the process. In this journey, fathers learn to find joy in each day, no matter what it brings.

As children grow and eventually leave the nest, fathers find themselves reflecting on the legacy they've built. They look back at the years spent together, at the laughter, the tears, and the countless memories made. They begin to understand that the true measure of fatherhood isn't in the material successes or the goals they once had, but in the love they gave and the person their child has become. Fatherhood is a journey that lives on, continuing to shape future generations through the lessons, values, and love passed down.

In these moments of reflection, fathers realize that they have given their children the most important gifts: the kinds of gifts that can't be touched, but felt. They see how their role has shaped not only their children's lives but their own as well. Fatherhood has changed them, deepened their capacity for love, and brought a profound sense of purpose. Through their guidance, fathers leave a legacy that echoes through the lives of their children and, eventually, their grandchildren. It is a legacy built on love, sacrifice, and intentional presence.

The journey of fatherhood is one that never truly ends. Even as children grow up and leave the home, a bond remains that was built from years of shared experiences. Fathers know that, though their children may go on to lead their own lives, a part of them will always be there as a gentle guiding presence, a memory of love and strength, a quiet voice reminding them of home. Looking back on the journey of fatherhood, a man can find peace in knowing that he has given his best, and that he is leaving behind a legacy that will live on in the hearts of those he loves.

Fatherhood is not a job with an end date; it is a lifelong commitment that only deepens with time.

To all the fathers who have dedicated their lives to loving, teaching, and shaping their children, you are the unsung heroes of everyday life. Your impact is immeasurable, your love is irreplaceable, and your role is truly the greatest job in the world.

A Love Letter to My Children

Dear Children,

As I sit here, surrounded by a half-finished bottle of Diet Dr. Pepper and a suspiciously missing remote, I can't help but reflect on the wild, beautiful rollercoaster ride it has been being your dad. Let me tell you, being your dad has been the greatest adventure of my life—and I'm talking about Indiana Jones-level adventure, complete with thrills, the occasional disaster, and moments of pure gold.

From the moment you burst into this world (loud, hungry, and already in charge), my heart ignited with a love so big I'm still trying to figure out how it fits in one chest. You didn't come with an instruction manual, which, frankly, was rude of you, but together we figured it out. Watching you grow, learn, and occasionally test the very limits of my sanity has been a privilege. Every milestone—from your first steps to the time you figured out sarcasm and used it against me—has been etched into my memory like my favorite dad jokes: unforgettable and usually embarrassing.

Let's not sugarcoat it: we've had our moments. There has been laughter so loud we cried, tears so big we crumbled, and moments when we looked at each other like, "How did we even get here?!" I've learned so much from you—patience (especially when you lost your shoes for the fifth time), compassion (even when I've stepped on LEGO bricks), and the kind of love that makes you want to do anything to see that person smile.

To my teenagers navigating the maze of adolescence: hang in there. Yes, I know, I'm old and "don't get it," but let me tell you a secret—I DO get it. I've been there. Trust me when I say the awkward phases, weird hairstyles, and questionable decisions are just pit stops on the road to greatness.

To my adult kids out there forging your own paths: you're crushing it. You might stumble, fall, or feel lost sometimes, but you're stronger than you think and smarter than you know. And hey, when life gets tough, remember you can always come back to the guy who'll still offer unsolicited advice and a cold Diet Dr. Pepper.

Here's the deal: life isn't a perfect script. It's messy, hilarious, and sometimes downright confusing. But if there's one thing I hope you always remember, it's this: kindness matters, integrity is non-negotiable, and perseverance will take you further than you think. Chase your dreams with everything you've got—and if those dreams don't work out, don't worry. We'll brainstorm a new one together.

Thank you for being the best kids a dad could ask for—for challenging me, teaching me, and giving me the world's best title: DAD. I'm always here, whether you need advice, a terrible pun, or just someone to remind you how proud they are of YOU.

With all the love and dad jokes in the world,

Dad

Acknowledgments

I would like to extend my heartfelt thanks to Ruben Garcia and Kelly Kendall from Utah State University. Your support, collaboration, and countless hours of conversation have been invaluable to me in our work with justice-involved fathers. I am grateful to have been on this journey with you both; the insights and experiences we have had together have left a lasting impact on me. Your commitment to our shared mission has been instrumental in bringing this work to life. I also wish to thank the Family Studies & Human Development Department at Utah State University for their steadfast support throughout this journey.

About The Author

R. Jack Eves Jr. is a dedicated educator, devoted family man, and passionate advocate for intentional fatherhood. Married to the love of his life, Gina, Jack cherishes every moment with his family, including their three wonderful children: Natasha, Hayden, and Jackson. With a career in education spanning more than 25 years, Jack has left a lasting impact on countless young lives, having taught middle school students across 6th, 7th, 8th, and 9th grades, and later stepping into roles as an Assistant Principal and High School Principal.

Beyond the walls of the classroom, Jack's commitment to family and community extended to his work with Utah State University, where he served in the Department of Human Development and Family Studies as a fatherhood coordinator. In this role, Jack developed and taught classes specifically designed for justice-involved fathers, supporting them in reconnecting with their families and becoming positive role models for their children. Now, as the Assistant Director of the Head Start program at Southern Utah University, Jack continues to foster growth and development in young people's lives, working tirelessly to ensure that every child has the foundational support they need for a bright future.

Jack's wealth of experience, both personal and professional, has shaped his approach to fatherhood, education, and leadership. His work stands as a testament to his belief that every child deserves guidance, every father deserves a chance to connect, and every family deserves to feel healthy and supported.

Made in the USA
Middletown, DE
01 December 2025

23533391R00055